Sew & Play

Enchanted Forest Toys

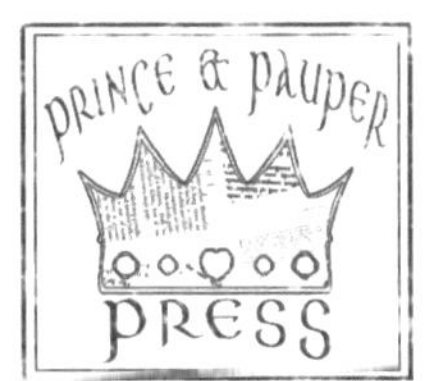

Jennifer Carson

Published by Prince & Pauper Press

Attention Teachers: The publisher and author encourage you to use this book as a text for teaching.

ISBN: 978-1-62251-041-2

Printed in the United States of America

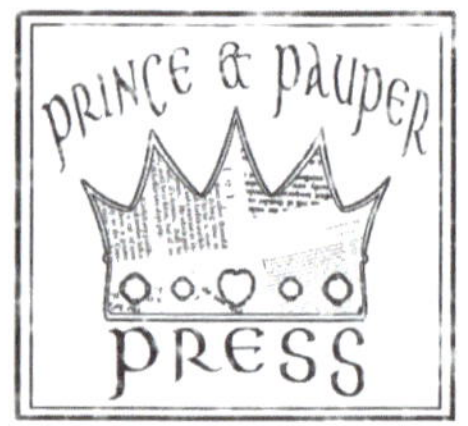

The Dragon Charmer

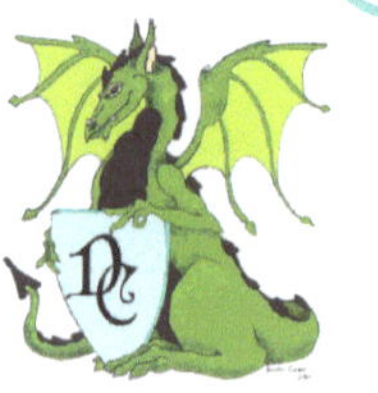

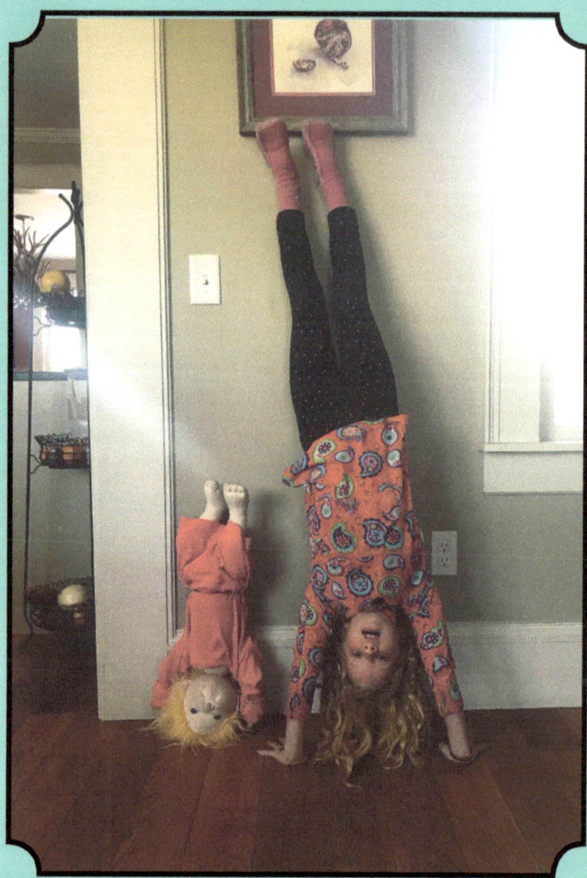

This book is dedicated to Catherine Vierzen. A faerie child who lives in the Great North Woods amongst the mountain trolls and porcupine dogs.

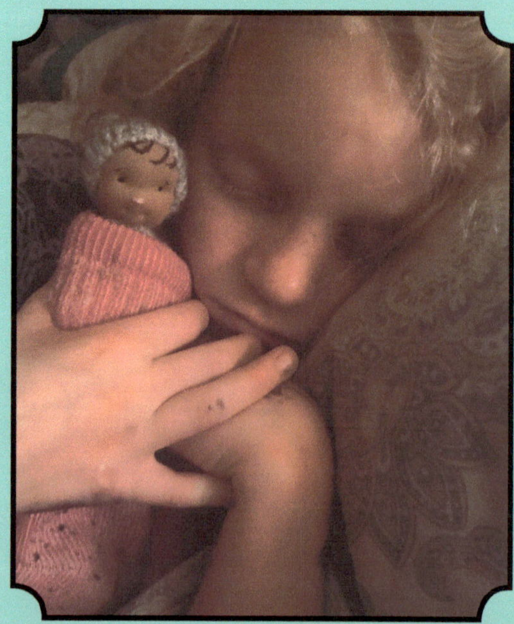

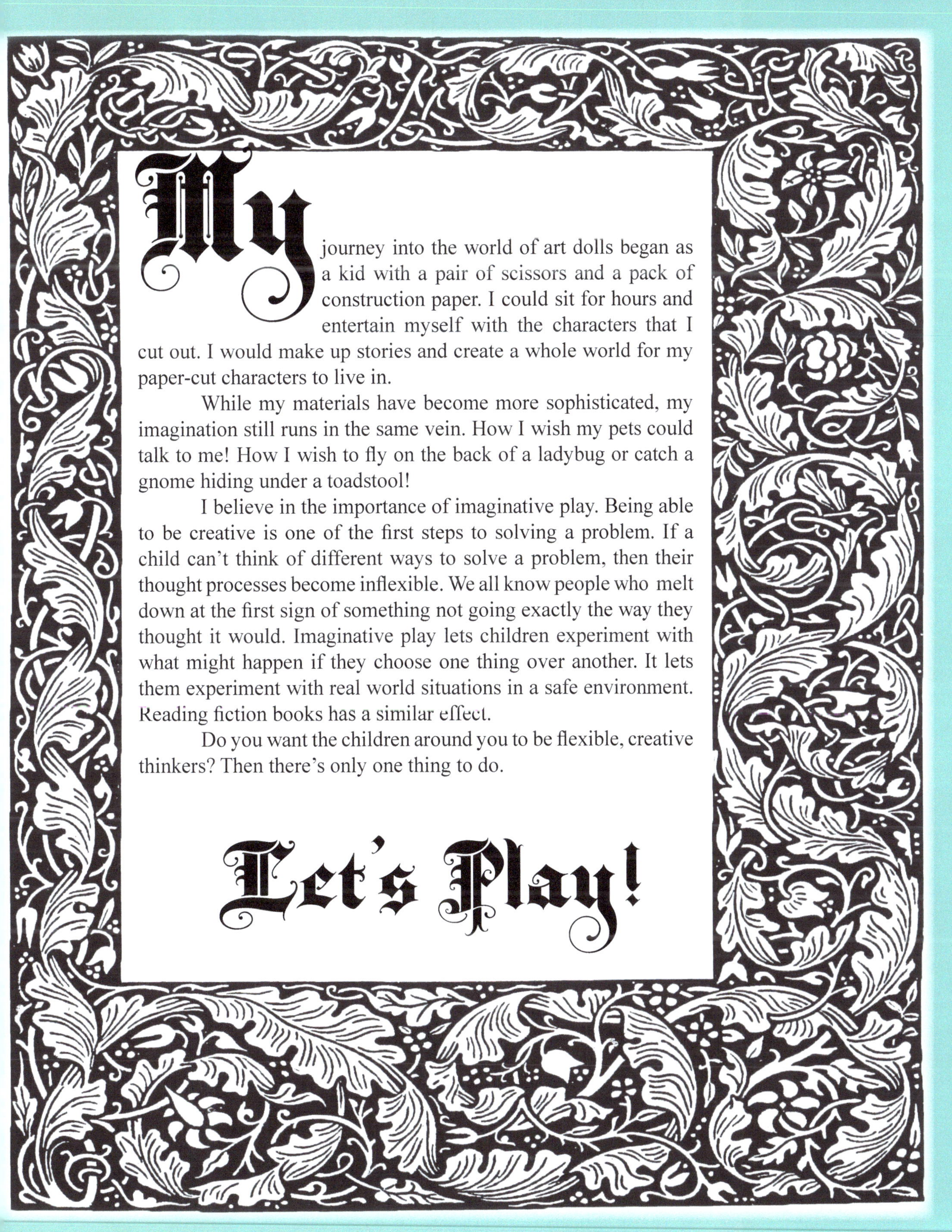

My journey into the world of art dolls began as a kid with a pair of scissors and a pack of construction paper. I could sit for hours and entertain myself with the characters that I cut out. I would make up stories and create a whole world for my paper-cut characters to live in.

While my materials have become more sophisticated, my imagination still runs in the same vein. How I wish my pets could talk to me! How I wish to fly on the back of a ladybug or catch a gnome hiding under a toadstool!

I believe in the importance of imaginative play. Being able to be creative is one of the first steps to solving a problem. If a child can't think of different ways to solve a problem, then their thought processes become inflexible. We all know people who melt down at the first sign of something not going exactly the way they thought it would. Imaginative play lets children experiment with what might happen if they choose one thing over another. It lets them experiment with real world situations in a safe environment. Reading fiction books has a similar effect.

Do you want the children around you to be flexible, creative thinkers? Then there's only one thing to do.

Let's Play!

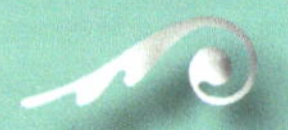

Contents

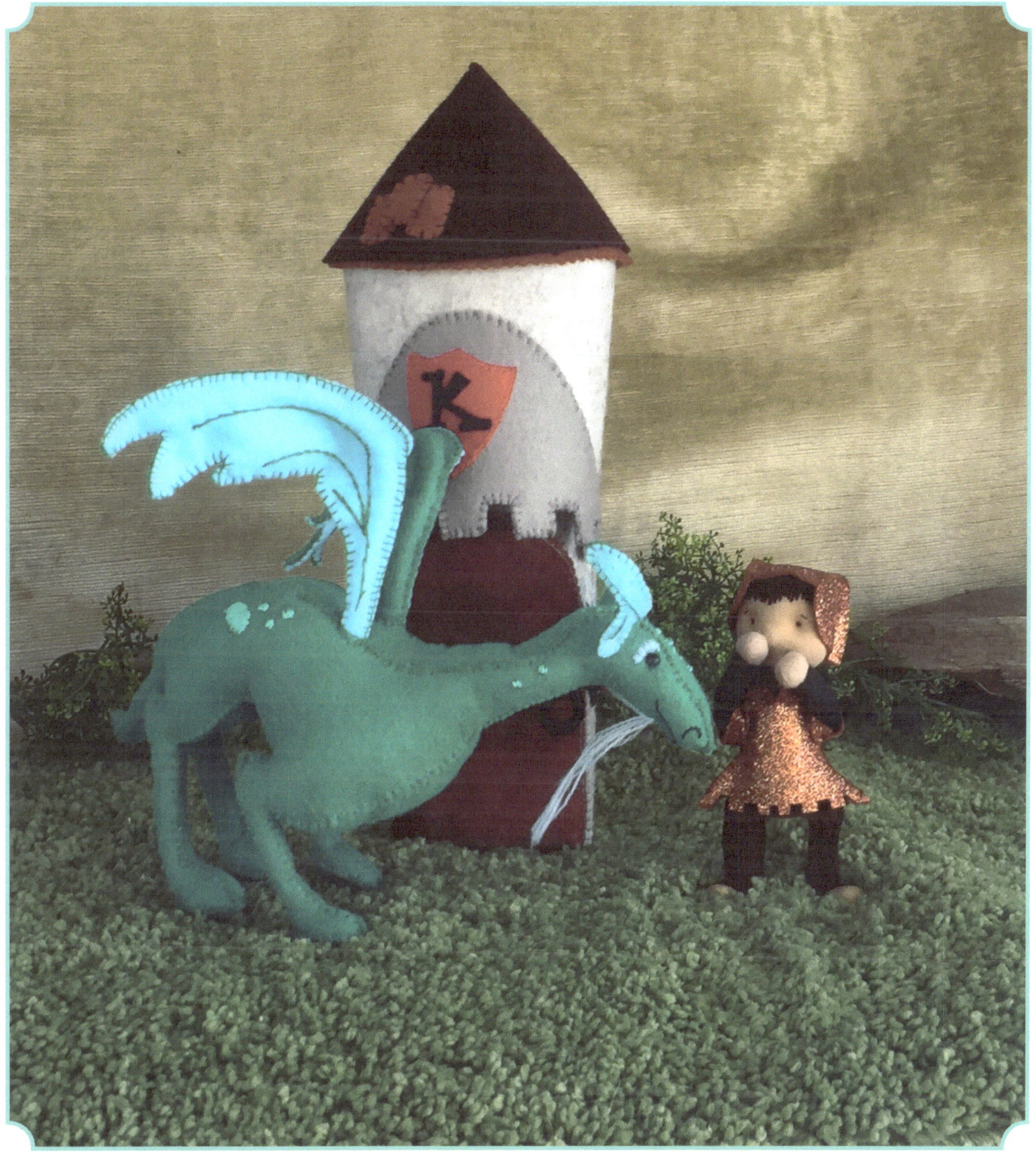

Oh no! A Dragon! I hope he's friendly...

Gather Your Materials

The Basics:

Some hand sewing basics are needed for the projects in this book. Most of these supplies can be found in any of your local craft stores or online. Some of the more hard to find supplies I carry in my Etsy shop. Look for a list of suppliers on page 74.

Tools:

- Small sharp scissors
- Wire cutters
- Round nose pliers (usually found in the jewelry section)
- Needles
- Freezer paper
- Japanese bunka brush
- Aileen's Tacky Glue
- Iron
- Pencil
- Small stuffing fork
- Measuring tape

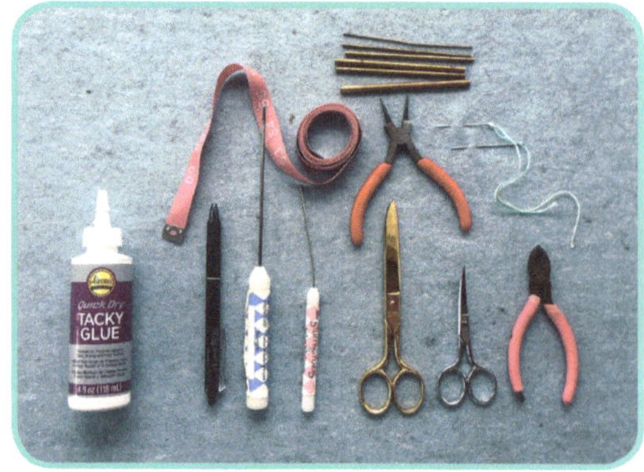

The tools you will need for the projects in this book. Don't forget the freezer paper (not pictured).

Materials:

Commonly Used Threads:

- Embroidery Floss and Genziana wool sewing thread
- A strong binding thread used for making Waldorf dolls.
- Upholstery thread—a strong polyester thread that I like to use for creatures that will be brushed out and made furry with the bunka brush.
- Wool stuffing

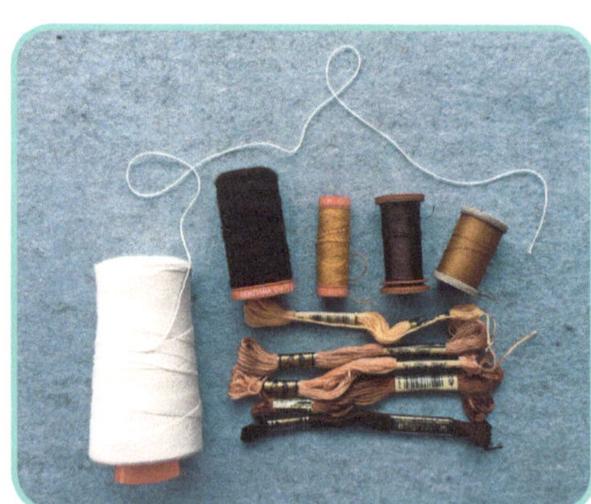

Commonly Used Fabrics:

- Wool Felt—there are two kinds of felt I prefer to use. National Non-Wovens WoolFelt®(Style WCF003) and De Witte Engel's CertiFelt in 3mm thickness. The CertiFelt is great for animals that you want to make fuzzy with the bunka brush because it is thicker than the wool felt from National Non-Wovens. Both companies offer different styles of wool felt in great colors.

- Cotton Plush Velour—is a nice fabric to use for clothes and comes in a great variety of colors. Sewing stitches sink in nicely.

- Cotton Interlock knit—this is the fabric we will use to make the heads of our elves and dwarves.

- Inner head tubing—comes in a lighter cotton gauze and a heavier cotton stockinette. The gauze works fine for the smaller dolls, and the stockinette doesn't tend to come in the smaller width needed for the dolls in this book, but if making larger dolls it is nice to work with. For the projects in this book we will use the 7/8" wide cotton gauze.

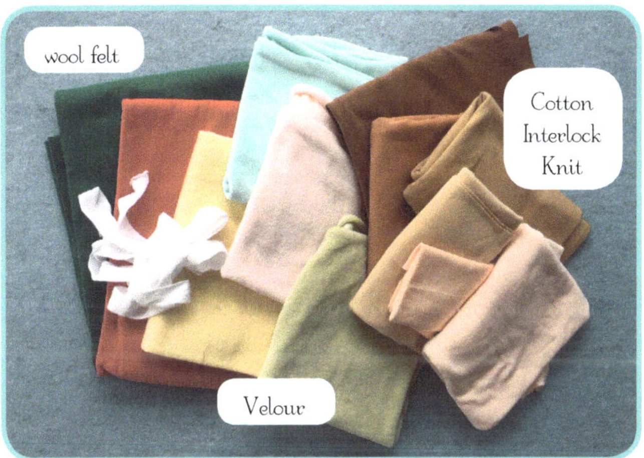

Inner head tubing in a cotton gauze is used to help shape small doll heads.

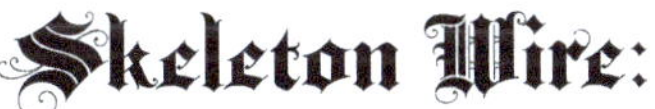

Skeleton Wire:

- Cloth covered floral wire for toes and hands
- De Witte Engel's Figure Cord
- Cotton pipe cleaners—also known as chenille stems

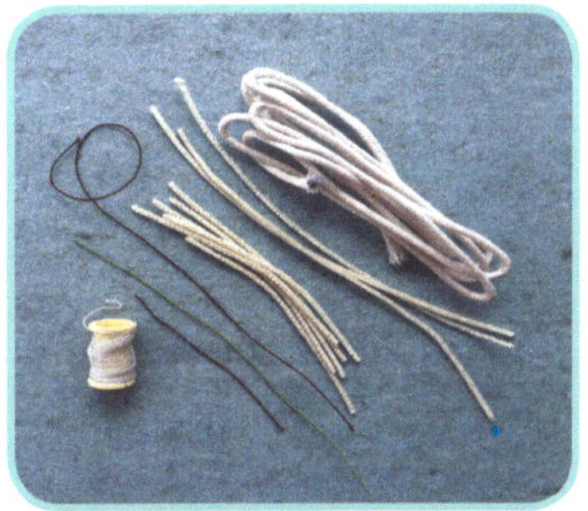

We will use three different types of wire for the projects in this book.

Eyes:

- Black seed beads in varying sizes for eyes
- Sew on eyes in 5 mm size
- Mini safety lock eyes (with backs!)
- Embroidering or needle felting eyes is always an option too!

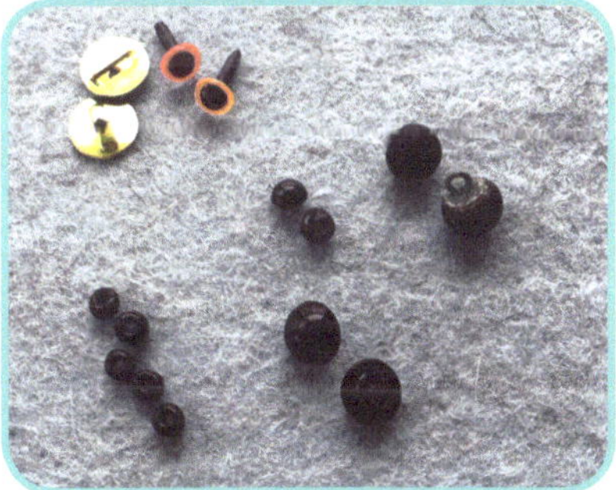

Eyes can be made from a variety of materials including:
safety lock eyes
seed beads
sew on eyes
vintage shoe buttons

Other Supplies:

- Angelina Film
- Prismacolor pencils for blushing cheeks & noses
- Tiny buttons and trims
- Wool felt balls (5mm and 10mm)
- Assorted hair fibers and yarns
- Bunka Brush (also known as a nap riser)

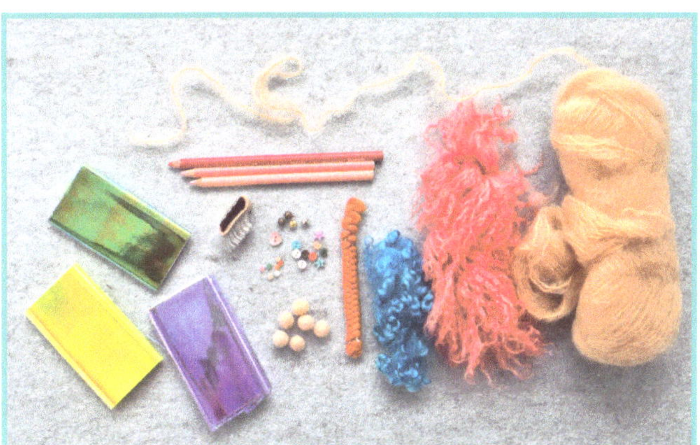

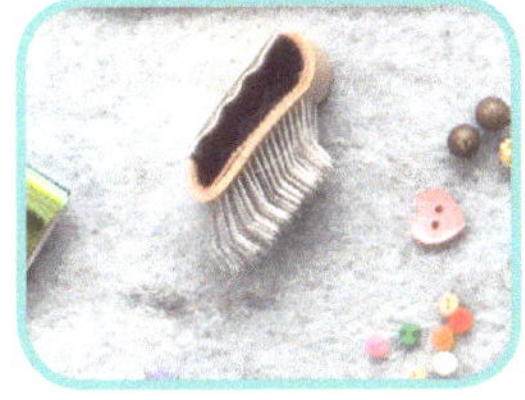

A bunka brush, pictured to the left, is a little brush that fits on your finger. It has metal combs that raise the nap of your material and makes yarn or floss, fuzzy.

Building Basics

Making the Pattern Pieces

You will want to trace any pattern pieces that will be cut from felt onto freezer paper for more precise cutting. Freezer paper has a shiny side and a paper side. You will draw on the paper side. Once you have all your pieces drawn and labeled on your freezer paper cut them out near the lines, but not on the lines, and separate them by what color they will be.

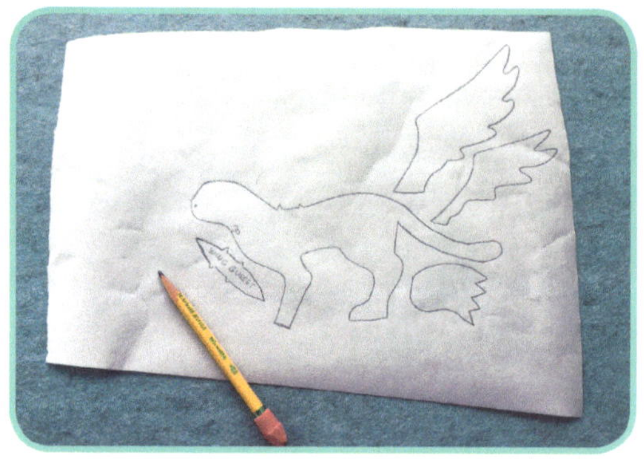

Draw your pattern pieces on the paper side of freezer paper with a pencil.

Arrange your pieces onto the correct color, shiny side down. With a warm iron, press the pieces onto your felt.

Once the paper is cool, cut the pieces out of your wool, right on the line. Peel your pattern off of the wool. Repeat steps to make any piece that needs two (or more, like the body or wings).

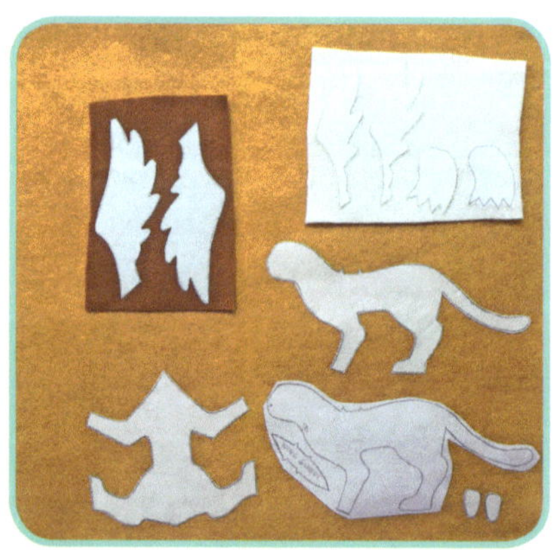

With a warm iron, press your pattern pieces onto the corresponding felt color.

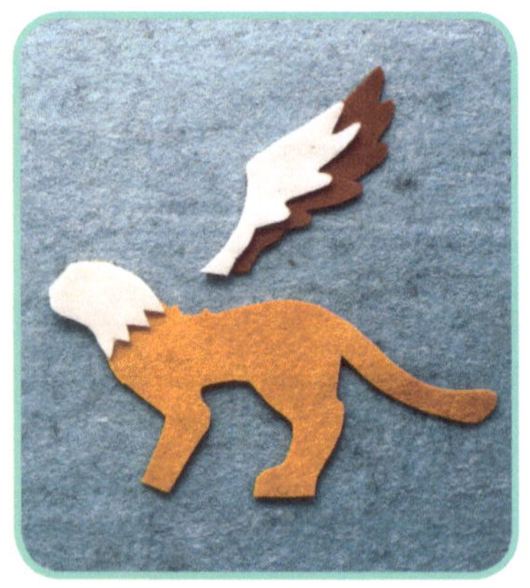

Cut all pieces out of felt with small, sharp scissors.

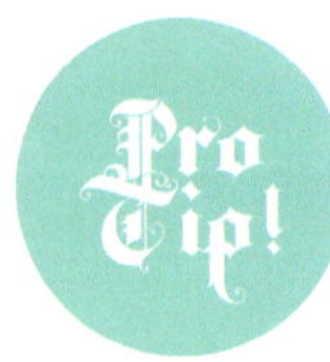

If you desire, you can trace two body pieces (or four wings) instead of reusing the freezer paper pattern.

Make the Skeleton

What follows are the basic general directions for making a skeleton for your posable creatures. For small creatures you may use chenille stems instead of figure cord. There may be more specific directions to follow in each project section.

1. Cut one piece of figure cord the length of the body, just short of the nose on one end, and just short of the tail end on the other. This is the spine of the body.

2. Pull back the fabric covering on each end and with your pliers, bend ¼" under so that the sharp end of the wires buries into the fabric covering. Wrap end with heavy thread and tie off.

3. Cut two more pieces of figure cord that will go from one foot to the other over the spine—cut it one inch longer than needed. One of these is the front legs, the other is the back legs. Bend each cord piece in half and bend ends as you did the spine.

4. Using the body pattern as a guide, slide one of the cord pieces down the spine so that it lines up with the front legs. Secure in place by sewing with your heavy thread.

5. Slide the other piece of cord up the spine from the tail end until it lines up with the back legs. Secure in place.

Before you get too much further, set your wire skeleton on top of one of your body felt pieces and bend to shape. Make sure that the fit is right. Make adjustments if needed. If your creature has a tail, it may not go all the way to the end as the tail end may be smaller than the figure cord. If you want the whole tail to be posable, you can add a length of chenille stem to the figure cord. Simply overlap the two wires and wrap with the binding thread.

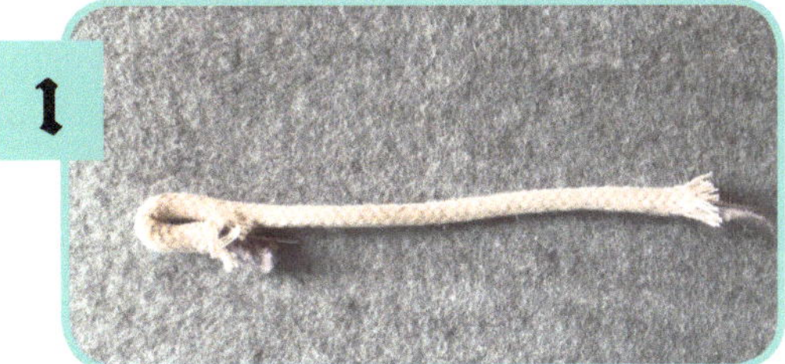

The spine of the skeleton.

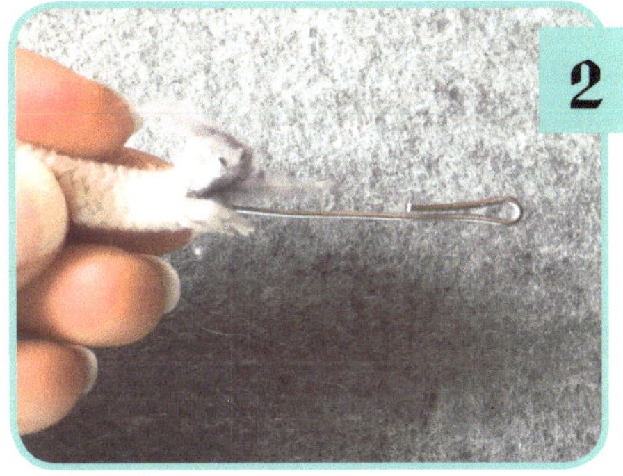

Pull the fabric covering back and bend the sharp wire over.

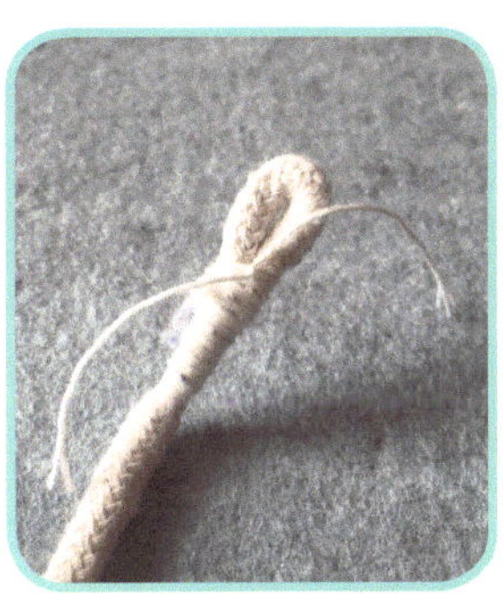

Wrap wire ends with heavy thread.

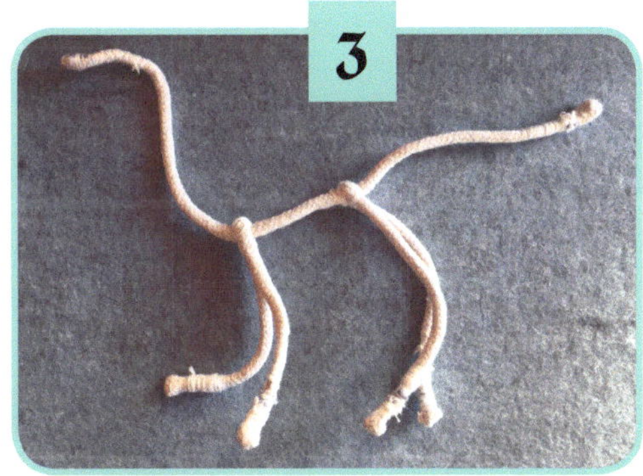

Cut wire for legs. Wrap the ends of the figure cord to pad sharp wire ends.

Now, bend each leg piece up ¼" so that the sharp end buries into the fabric covering as you did with the spine ends. Bend any extra fabric covering up and over the toes. Take a length of your binding thread and wrap the toes and up the leg toward the spine. Knot and bury thread end at top of leg. Repeat for each foot/leg. If you are working with a chenille stem skeleton part, you will still want to bend sharp end up, but you won't have the fabric covering to help pad the sharp point. Wrap some extra binding thread around it and make sure it is covered well.

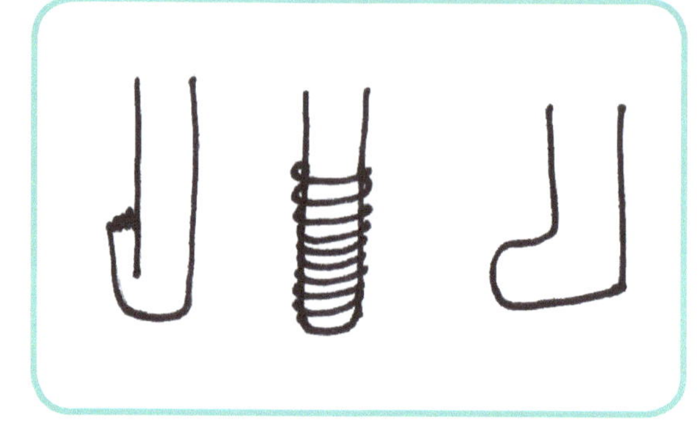

With your pliers, bend the end of the leg to make the foot.

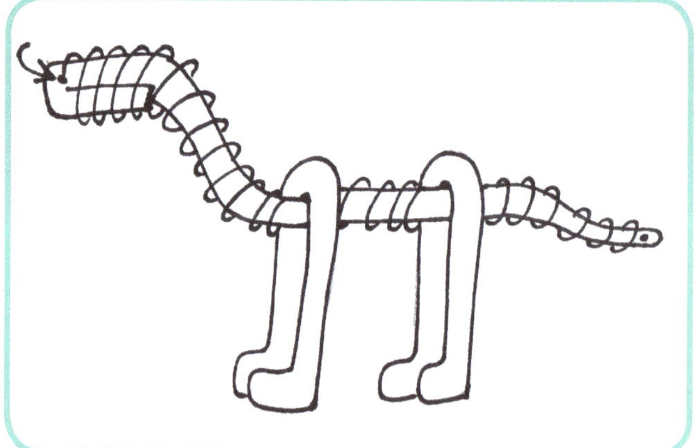

Optional: To really make a tight skeleton, anchor a length of binding thread in neck and then wrap the thread around the neck and down the spine toward the tail. Knot thread after wrapping tail. Clip end of thread.

With another length of heavy thread knot at point where the front legs cross over the spine. Wrap this joint tightly and tie off. Repeat for back legs.

If your creature has wings, you will cut and attach your figure cord in the same way you did the legs, (except pointing up!) using your pattern as a guide for placement.

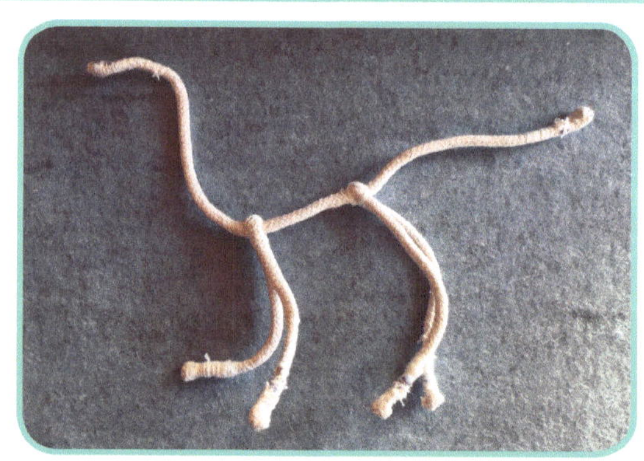

An example of a figure cord skeleton after being secured in place with the heavy thread. Above without wings, below, after wings were added.

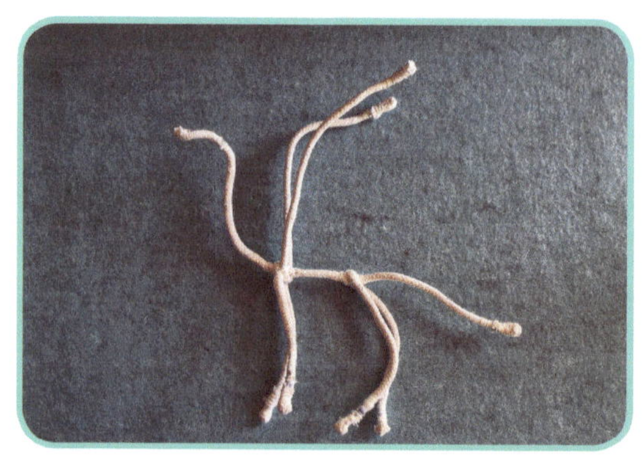

Pro Tip! You can also make skeletons for small creatures out of chenille stems, floral wire, or a combination. In this book we use the figure cord for the spine in the Gryphon, but chenille stems for his wings, tail, and legs, and floral wire for his front feet. Use what makes sense depending on the size of your creature.

Make the felt body:

If your gusset pattern has darts, begin by cutting out the darts. (A dart is a diamond or elongated oval cutout usually found in the belly gusset or armpit, but sometimes in the stomach or back pieces, depending on the pattern). Then, with RST, stitch darts closed with a whipstitch or tiny blanket stitch. This narrows the gusset a bit.

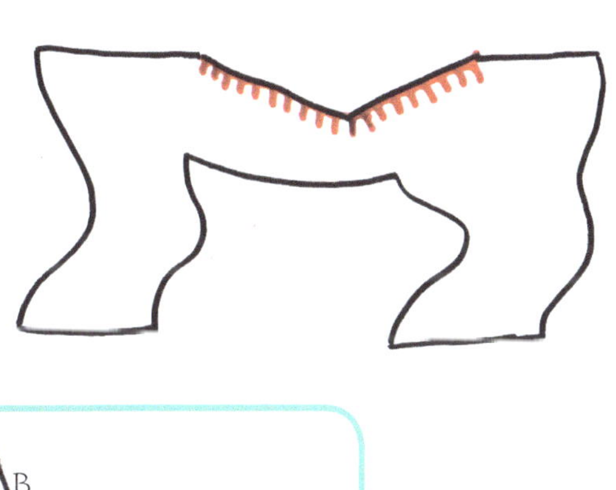

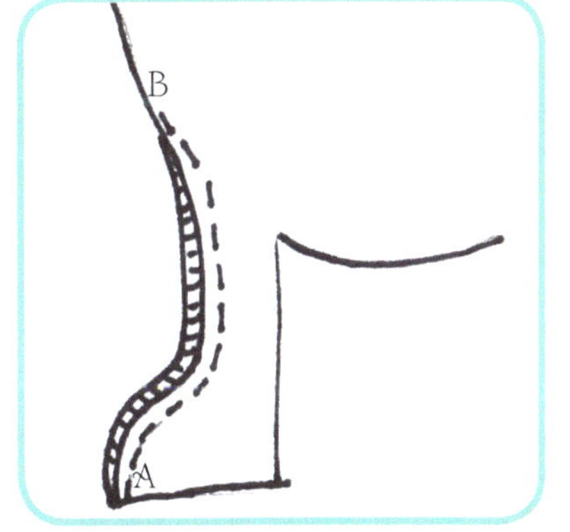

Match the front edge of the body gusset to one side of the body. Using your heavy upholstery thread or two strands of embroidery floss and a tiny blanket stitch, sew up the front side of the front foot (point A on the pattern pieces) and leg to the point of the belly gusset (point B on the pattern pieces).

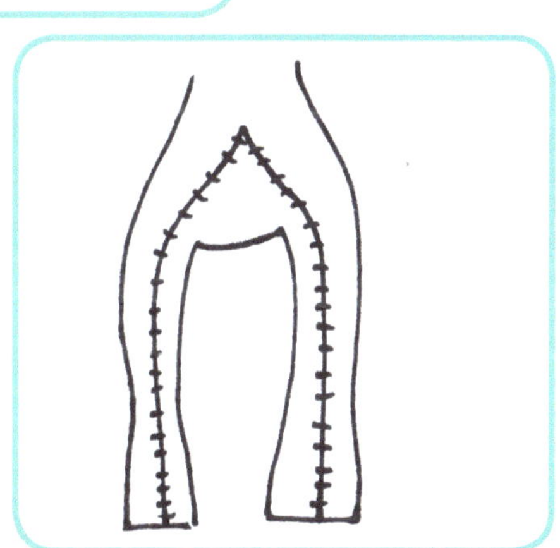

Match the front edge of the other side body to the other leg on the gusset. Stitch up to the point of the belly gusset. You should now have the front edges of the gusset sewn to the side body at the front of the legs.

Place the skeleton into the front of the body. For the Gryphon, his front feet will stick out of felt on the front legs.

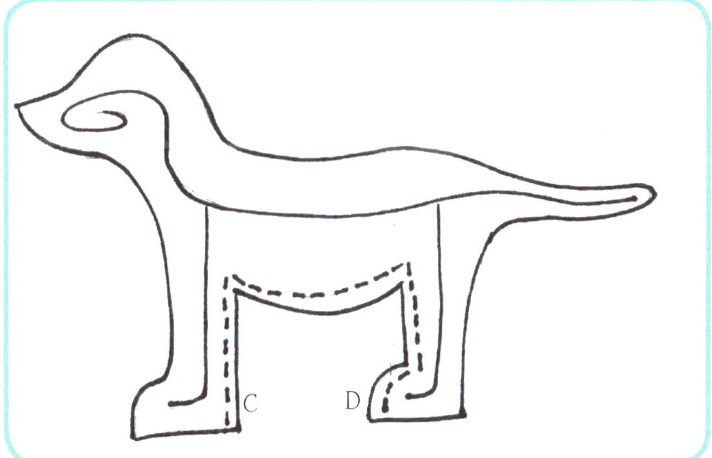

Stitch up the back of one leg (point C) and continue to stitch the belly gusset, across the belly, and down the front of the rear leg (point D).

Repeat for the other side of the body.

Now stitch the back side of the rear leg (point E) up to the point in the gusset (point F). If your creature has a long tail, the point of the gusset will reach down the tail about ¼".

Repeat for the opposite leg. When you reach the "point" of the gusset, continue sewing down the underside of the tail (if your creature has a tail) and around the tip. Stuff the end of the tail with your tiny stuffing fork.

Continue to sew the tail. Stop when you get about 1" past the top of the tail where it connects to the body (point G).

Stuff the bottom of the leg before stitching soles onto creatures that have narrow legs. Next stitch the soles of the feet in place with a tiny blanket stitch. Stuff the upper part of the legs with your tiny stuffing fork. Work with small pieces at first. You will have to manipulate the stuffing a little to get it under the spine. Don't stuff the body too much yet, let's get the head gusset (if your creature has one) sewn in first!

Match the center of the nose end of the gusset to the center seam of the face. To find the center, fold the gusset in half.

Starting at this center point, stitch the head gusset to the side of the head with tiny blanket stitches. Knot your thread when you reach the point of the gusset.

Beginning at the center again, stitch the other side of the gusset. When you reach the point of the gusset, continue down the neck about 1" (point H) and make a secure knot if your creature doesn't have wings. If your creature does have wings, knot your thread at the point where the wing skeleton will emerge from the body and skip to the **Adding Wings** section on next page.

From this point forward, you will stitch and stuff at the same time.

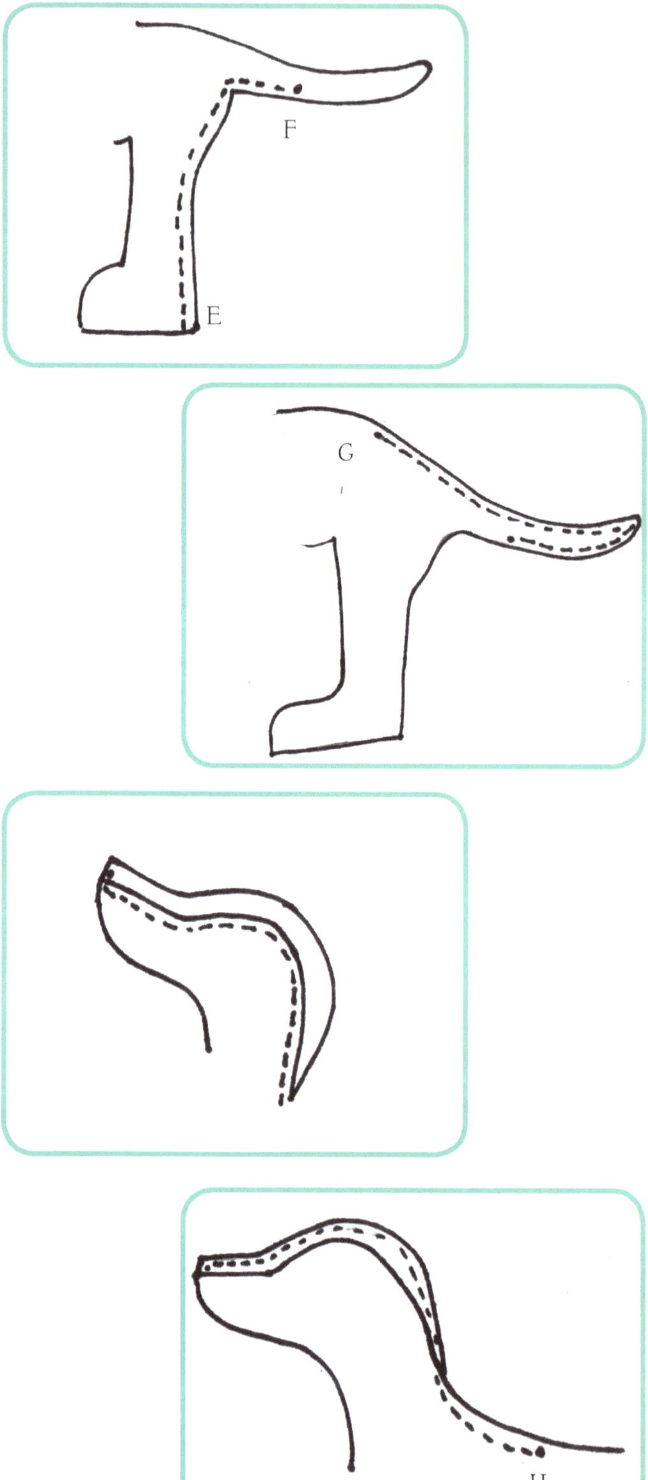

Stuff the head. Make it firm, but don't overstuff. You don't want to stress the seams.

Continue stuffing and sewing the back closed. When you are happy with the look and shape of your creature, and the back has been totally sewn up, knot your thread and bury the end.

For creatures with wings, see the Adding Wings section below.

Adding Wings

1. Stuff the head and neck. Make it firm, but don't overstuff. You don't want to stress the seams. Continue sewing down the neck and stuffing the body to the point where the wing gusset will be sewn in. Knot your thread.

2. Sew the top edge of two wings together from point "A" to point "B". Insert your figure cord skeleton, then continue stitching the outer edge of the wing. Knot and bury thread end.

3. Stitch wing gusset to body matching notches on body pattern (you will want to clip these notches off once you have pinned your gusset in place).

4. Using a tiny blanket stitch sew the gusset into the body. When you get to the point of where the wings meet the body, stitch the outer edge of the wing to the body and then continue to stitch the gusset in place. Repeat for the other outer side of the gusset. Knot thread and bury end.

5. Now you will need to stitch the inner part of the wing to the gusset as well. I have uploaded a video to my website showing how I sew the wing gusset in if you need more help to understand this process. Find the link in the resources section starting on page 74.

6. Embroider any bone lines on the wings as indicated on the pattern.

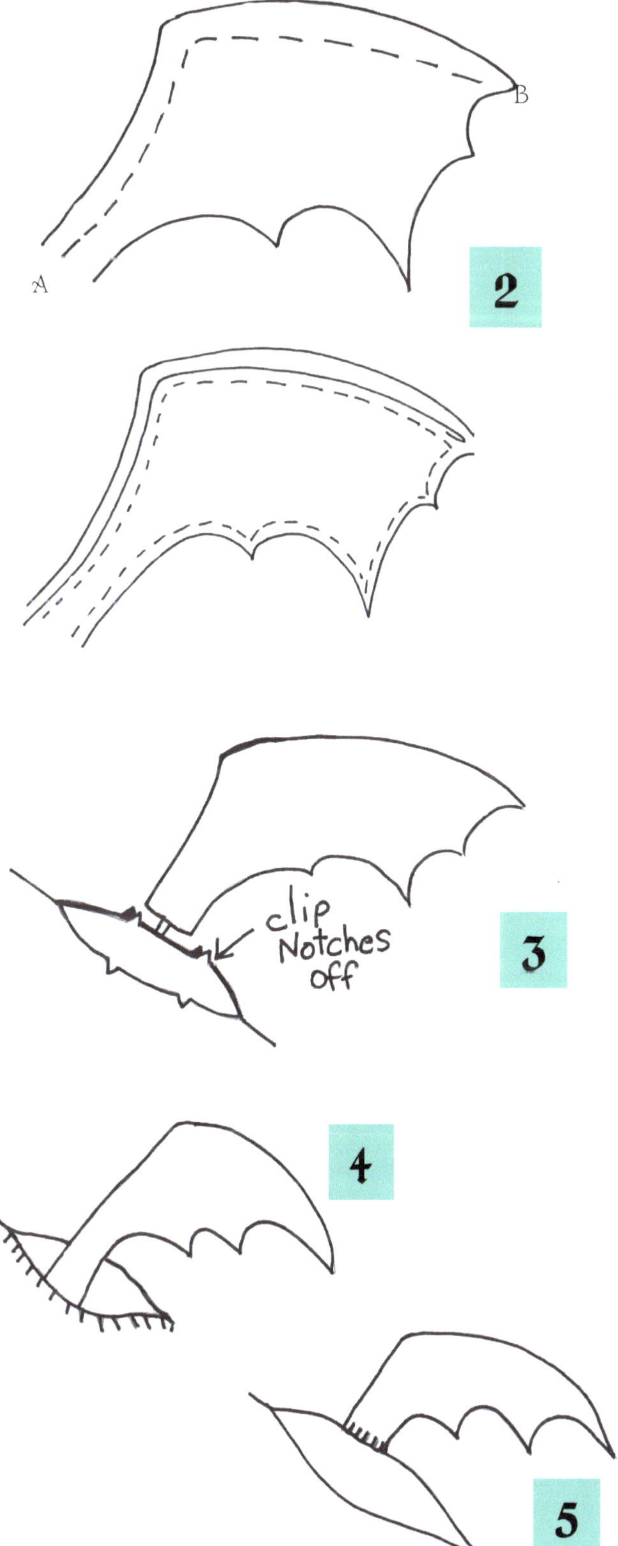

Adding Details:

Embroider any details like nostrils, spots, beards, ear detail lines, hair, eyebrows, mouth or tail tufts.

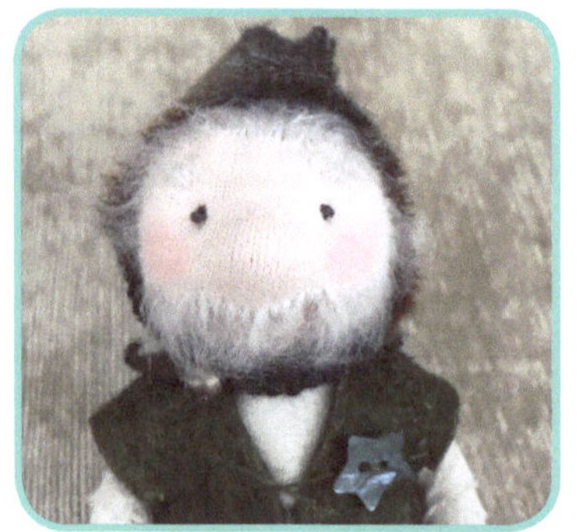

I used a white Genziana thread to embroider this Gnome's eyebrows, hair, and beard. Embroidering all his hair will take longer than you think, so have some patience. I then lightly brushed the threads with a bunka brush for a bit of a fuzzy look.

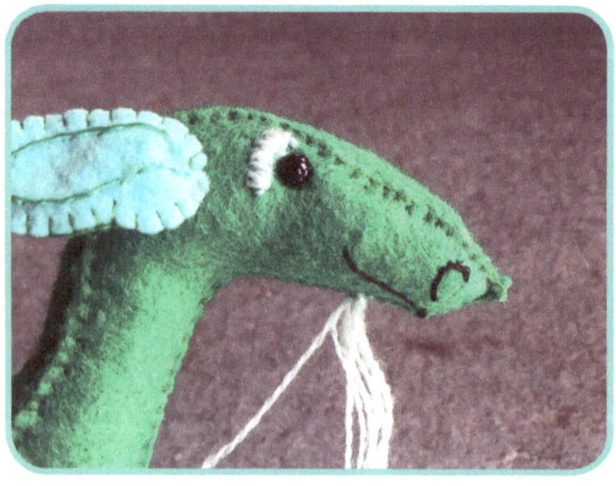

If you want a furry creature brush the felt with a Japanese bunka brush. Make sure to use a thicker felt and a light touch so that you don't wear holes into the felt.

To make a furry beard or eyebrows you could also embroider with wool tapestry yarn or wool sewing thread and then brush with the bunka brush, as pictured above. This is also the technique I used for giving the gryphon a tuft of hair on the end of his tail.

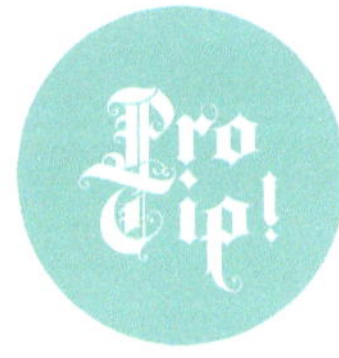

You can also pre-fur felt pieces before you sew them by brushing the pieces and then sewing them together. This is great for pieces that have tight curves, like under the neck.

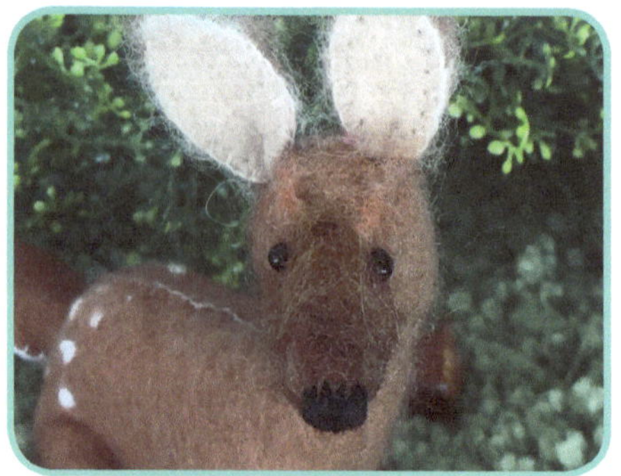

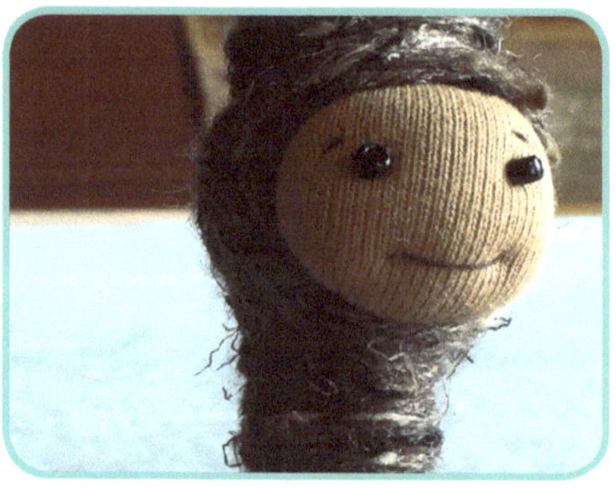

Seed beads are great for eyes if you are making creatures for children who don't put toys in their mouth anymore. You could also use small safety lock eyes or sew on eyes, or you could embroider the eyes. If you choose to use safety-lock eyes, you will need to put those in before you sew the body pieces together.

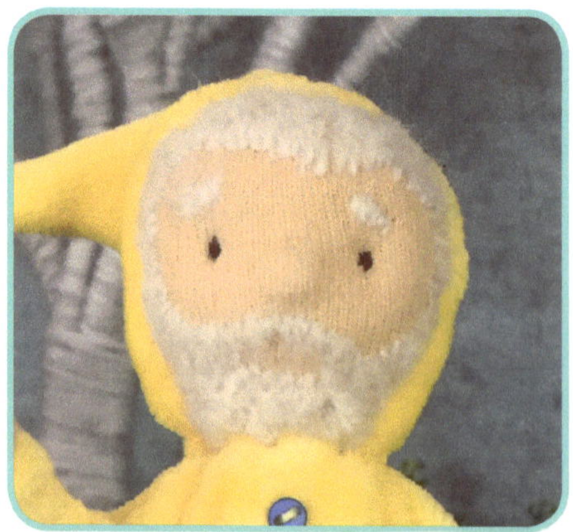

This Gnome has simple embroidered eyes.

The Projects

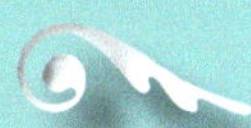

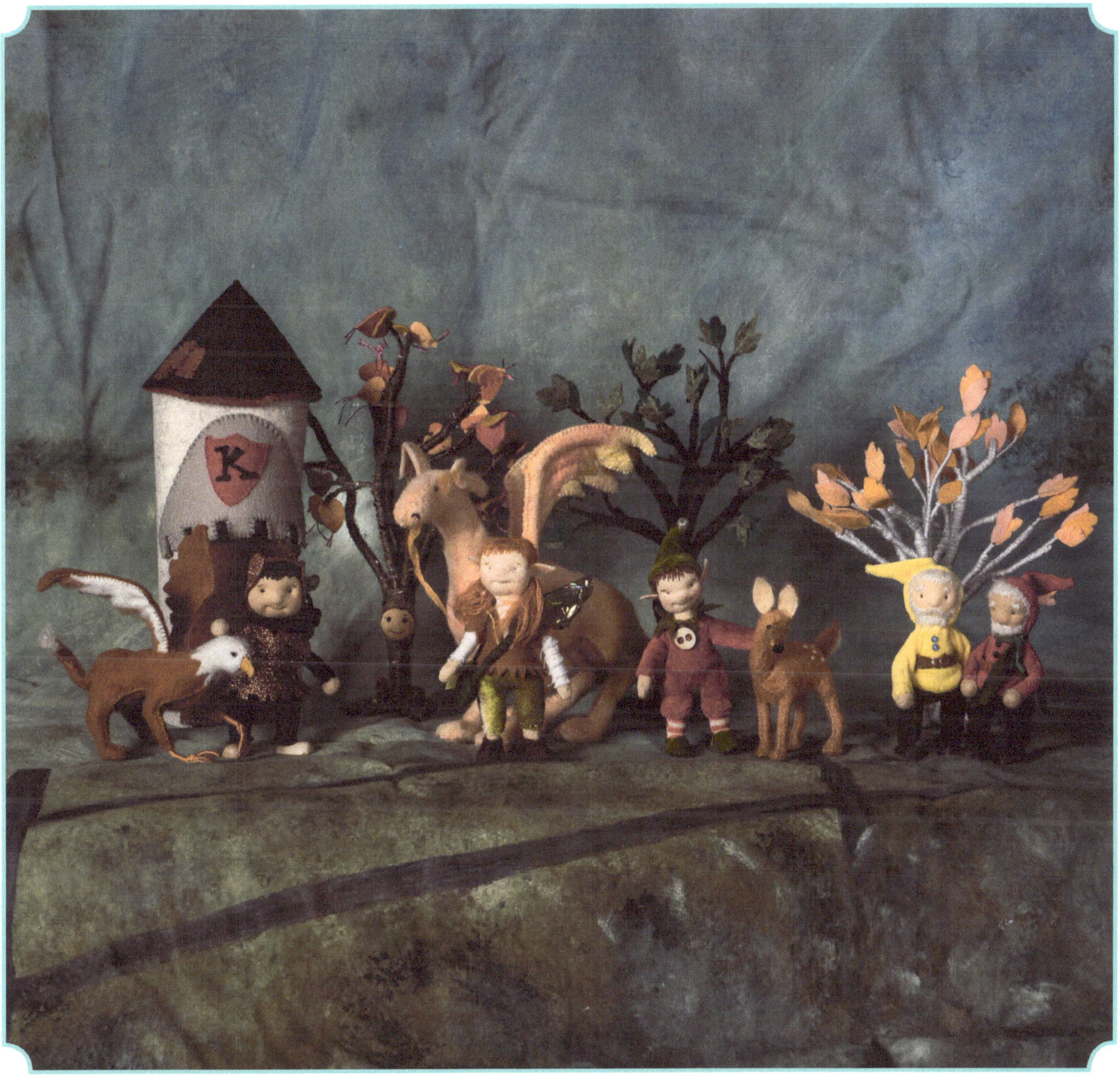

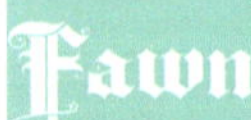

The fawn is a great chance to learn how to work small.
Use a chenille stem skeleton for the fawn.

Materials Needed:

- Wool felt in light brown, scraps of white, and tan
- White Genziana wool thread
- Embroidery floss to match body color and white
- Five 12" cotton pipe cleaners
- Wool stuffing
- Tools
- Basic sewing supplies (see page 6)

Cut out all your body pieces from your felt following the directions in the Making the Pattern Pieces section on page 8.

1. Layer the tan ear piece with the brown ear piece. You may wish to use a drop of fabric glue to keep in place. Stitch curved edges with a tiny blanket stitch and two strands of floss. Repeat for second ear.

2. Layer the white tail piece with the brown tail piece. Stitch curved edges with a tiny blanket stitch using two strands of white floss.

3. Make the skeleton using chenille stems following the general directions on page 9.

4. Sew the body together using the directions on page 11. The head gusset starts at the "X" as indicated on the body pattern instead of at the center seam on the nose.

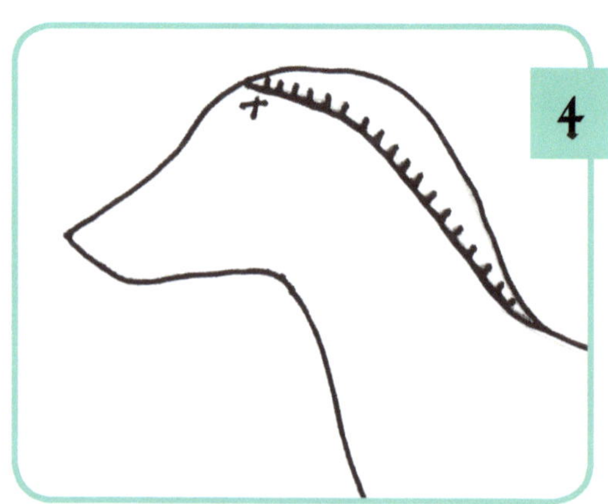

5. Embroider nose with black thread and sew in bead eyes or embroider eyes. Attach ears to top of head.

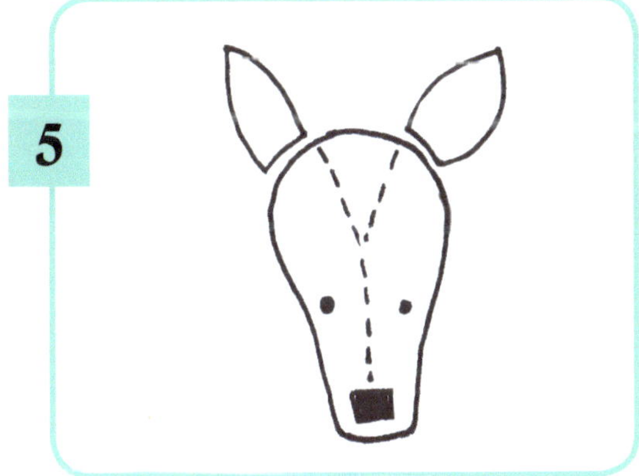

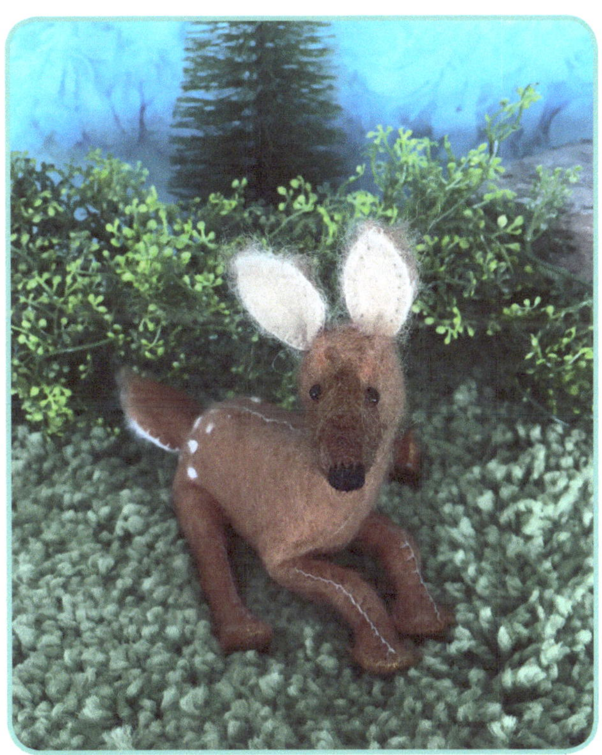

6. With white wool thread, embroider spots on her back and bottom. Attach tail to rear end.

7. Brush lightly with your bunka brush if you want her to look furry.

Pro Tip! Brush a little too much and now have a hole in your felt? Use some of the material that gathered in your bunka brush and needle felt it back in!

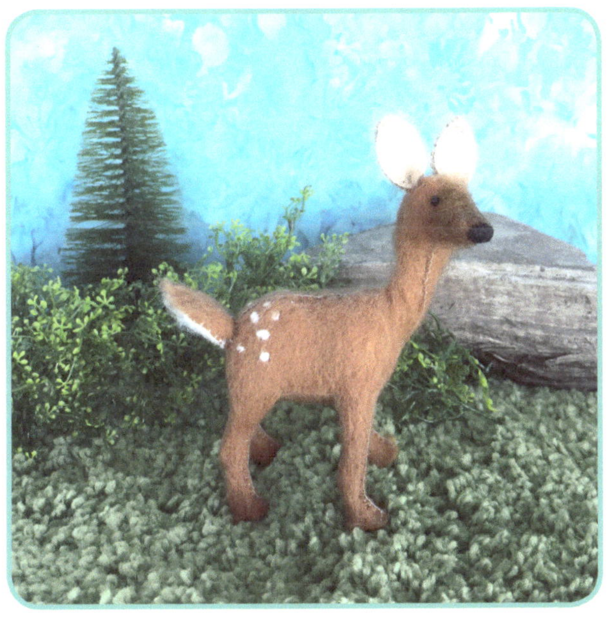

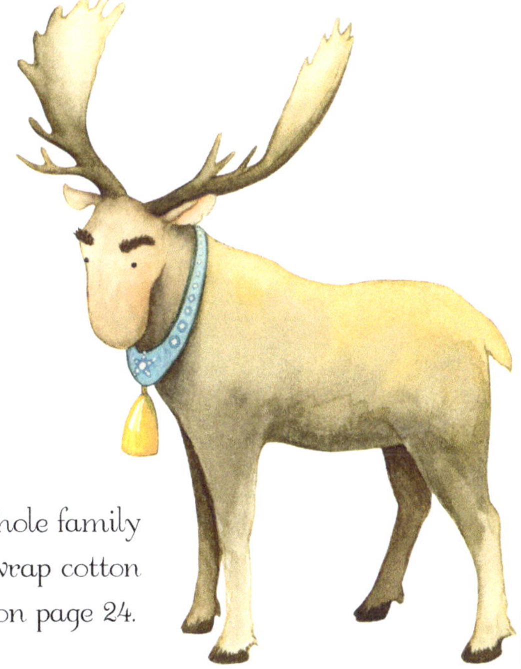

Pro Tip! You could enlarge the fawn pattern to make a whole family of deer! Cut antlers out of felt for the papa or wrap cotton pipe cleaners in floss. like in the Dryad pattern on page 24.

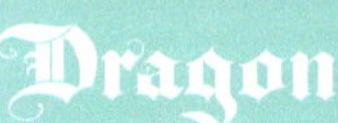

The dragon uses a simple figure cord skeleton with the added challenge of adding wings.

Materials Needed:

- Wool felt in your choice of color
- Wool thread, your choice of color for beard and eyebrows
- Embroidery floss to match body and black
- 48" of Figure cord
- Glass, or safety lock eyes (or you can embroider/needle felt eyes)
- Wool stuffing
- Tools
- Basic sewing supplies (see page 6)

Follow special directions on the pattern pieces to make full size pattern pieces. Cut out all your body pieces from your felt following the directions in the Making the Pattern Pieces section on page 8.

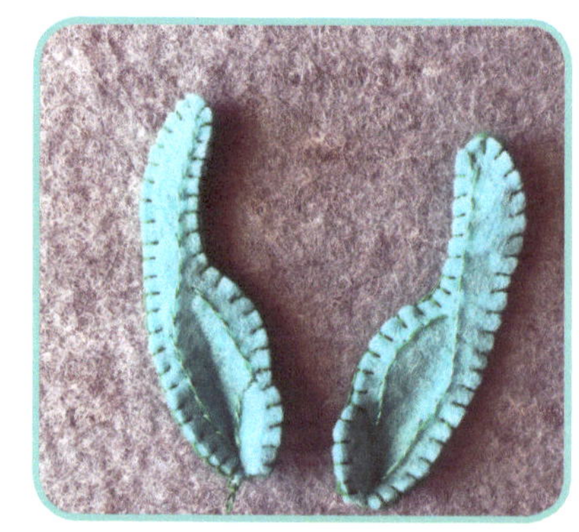

1. If desired, embroider ear following guide to the right for a bit of definition.

2. Make the skeleton using figure cord and following the general directions beginning on page 9.

3. Sew the body together using the directions beginning on page 11.

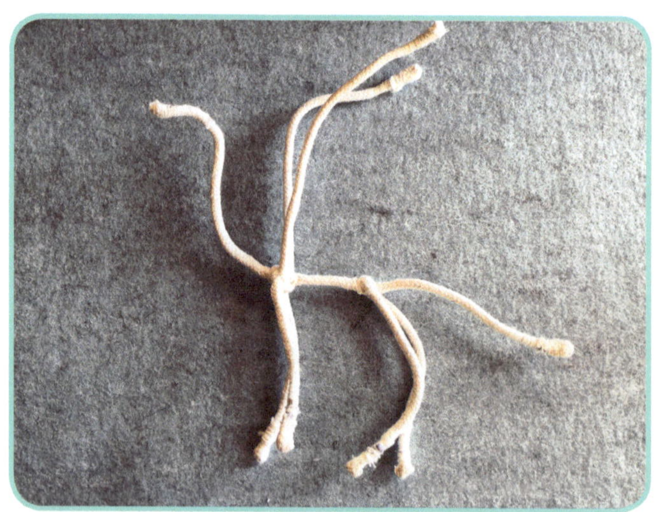

Dragon's completed skeleton

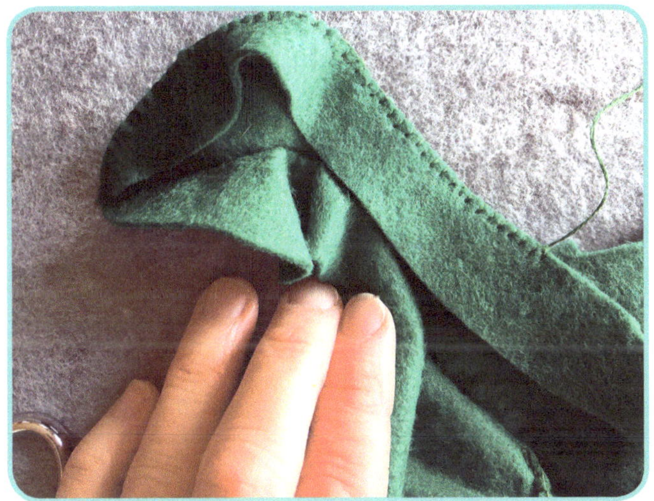

Sewing in the head gussett

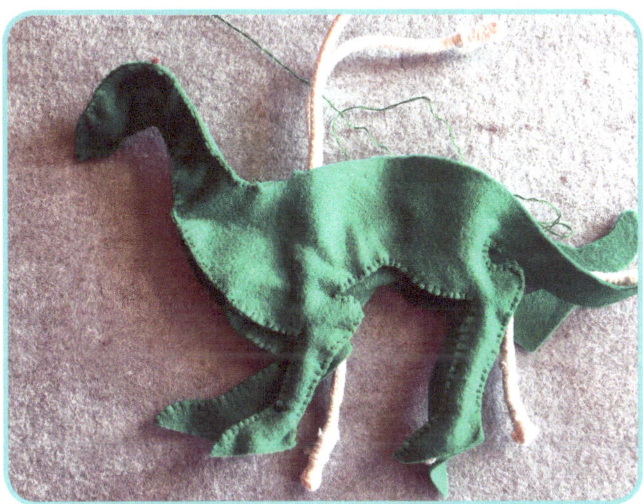

One side completely sewn with skeleton inserted.

☆ Note: Dragon's gusset begins at the center of his muzzle and continues down his back. It is one continuous gusset instead of having separate head and wing gussets.

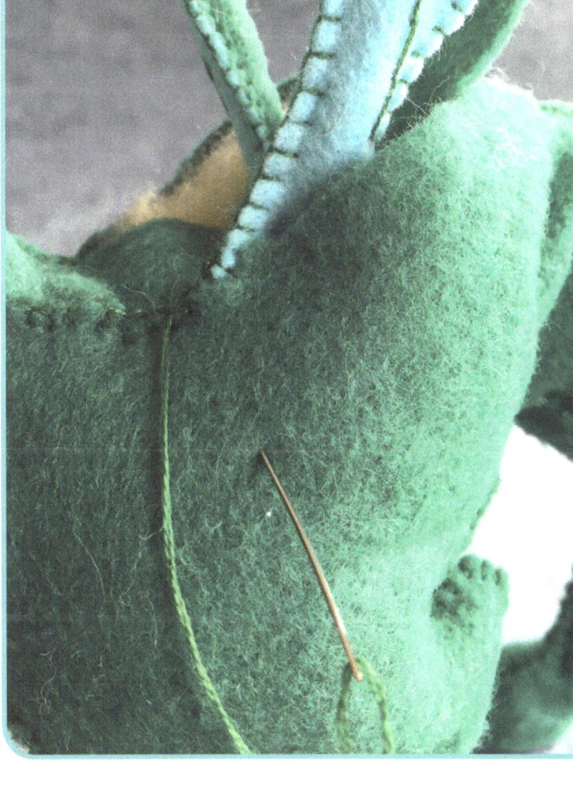

Finishing the other side of the gusset, moving toward the wing.

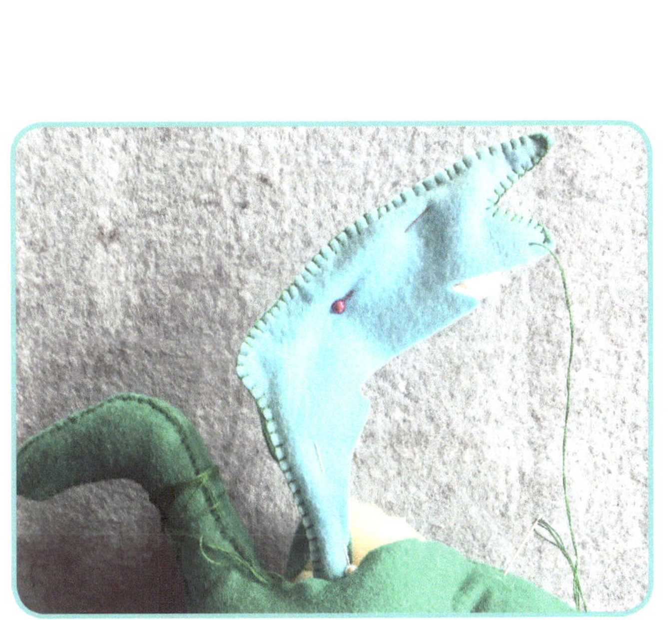

Wing top is sewn. Preparing to sew wing "bone" lines.

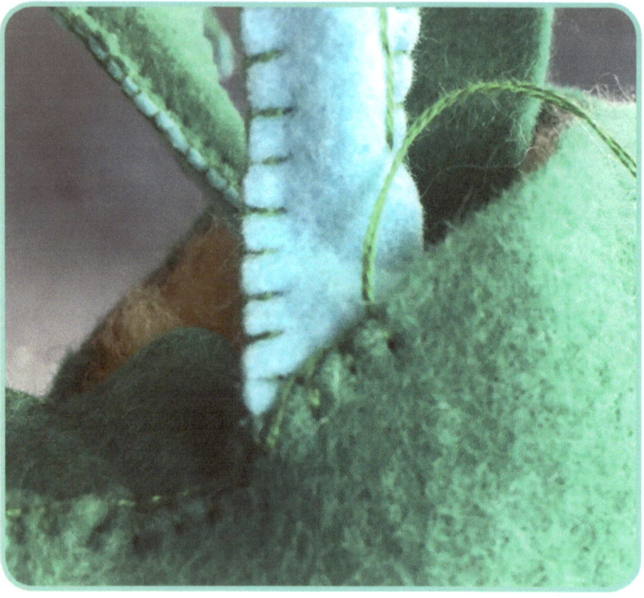

Sewing the body to the outside of the wing.

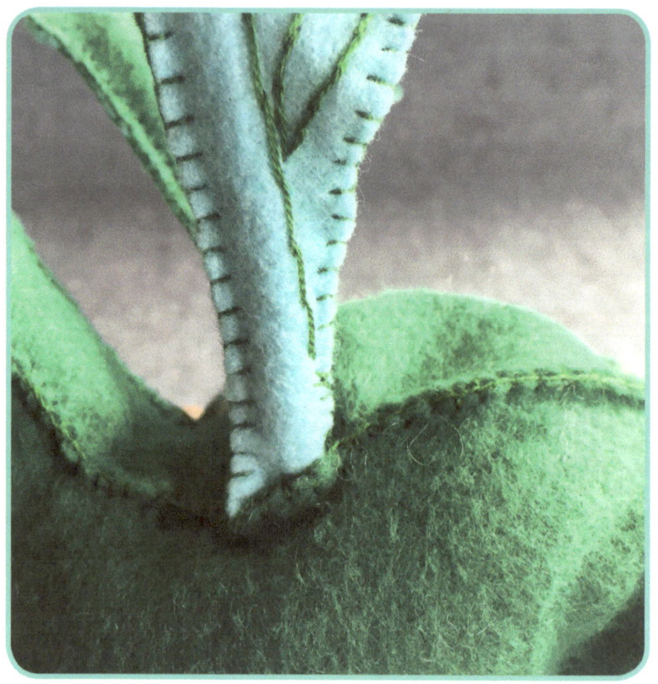

One side of the gusset is now finished.

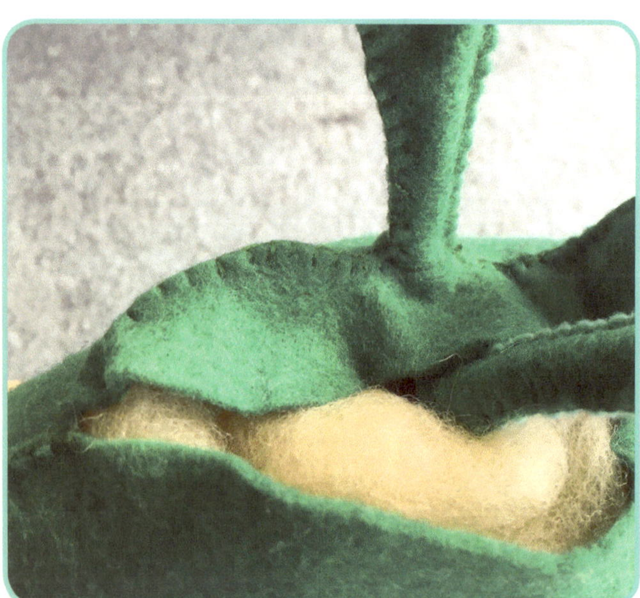

One side of the gusset finished--notice how the inside of the gussett is not sewn yet.

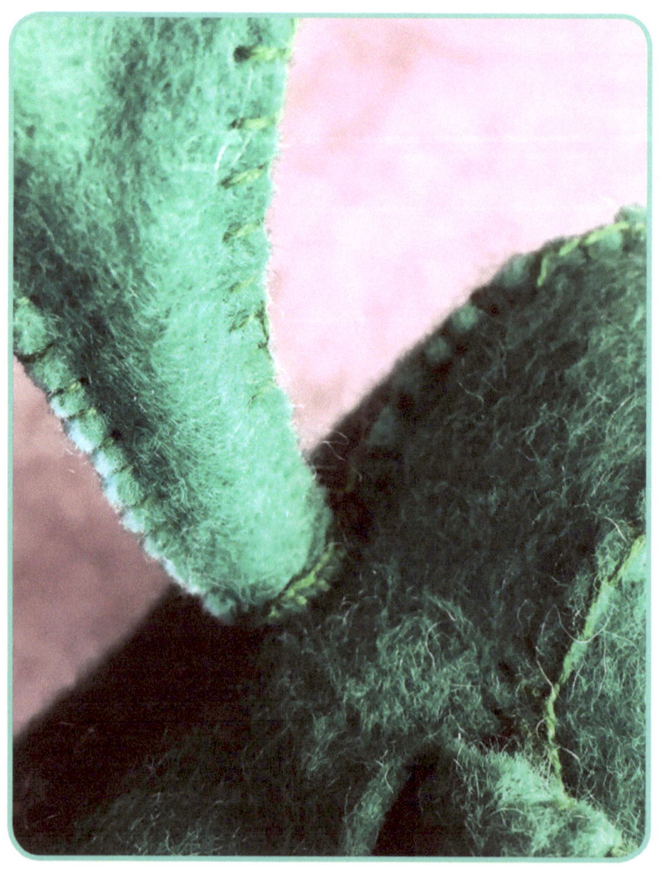

One gusset completed--notice how the inside of one gusset side is now sewn to the inside of the wing as well.

4. Once your dragon is stitched and stuffed, stitch on two seed beads for his eyes. You could also embroider or needle felt his eyes.

5. Embroider his nostrils and his mouth.

6. With your wooly thread, give him a beard and some fuzzy eyebrows. Comb them out a bit with your bunka brush.

7. If you desire, embroider or needle felt spots on your dragon.

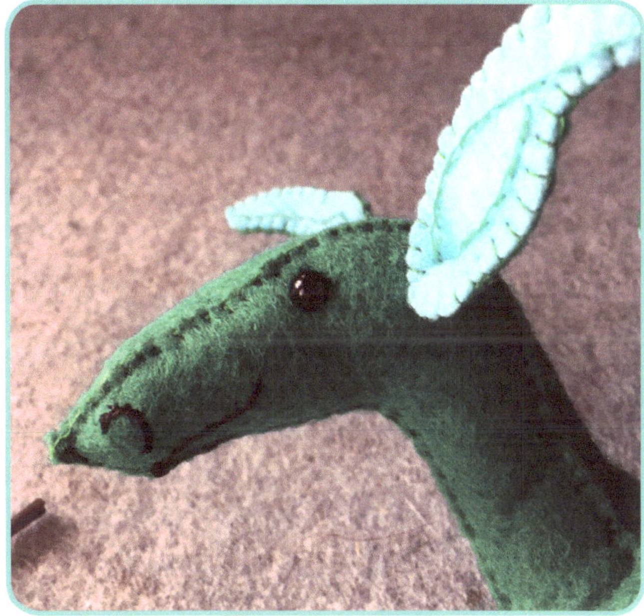

Embroider a mouth and nostrils with black thread. Sew in his eyes or embroider his eyes.

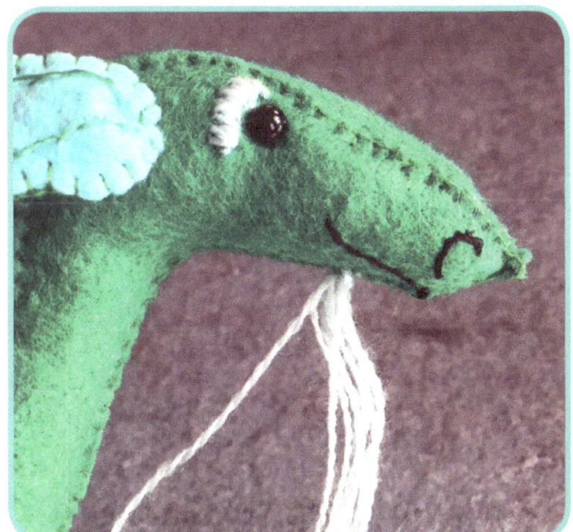

Using a wool blend thread, like Genziana, embroider his eyebrows and give him a beard.

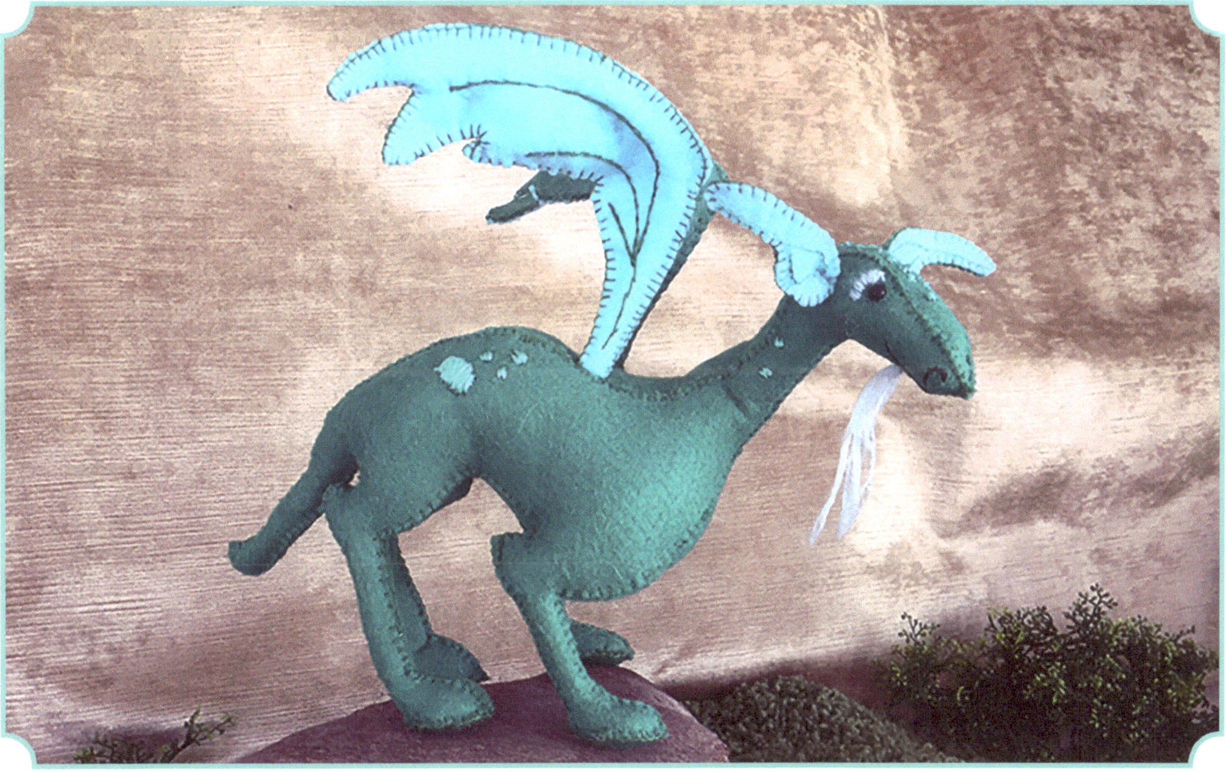

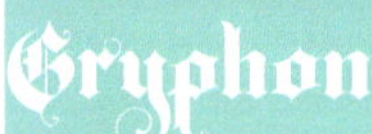

Gryphon

The Gryphon has a layered head and wings and features a combination body skeleton and wrapped wire feet.

Materials Needed:

- Wool felt in white, golden yellow, and reddish brown or color of your choice for body
- White Genziana wool thread
- Embroidery floss for toes in your choice of color
- 16” of figure cord
- Five 12” cotton pipe cleaners
- Cloth covered floral wire, two pieces 8 1/2” long
- Strong cotton thread
- Wool stuffing
- Tools
- Basic sewing supplies (see page 6)

★Note: There is no head gusset for the Gryphon

1

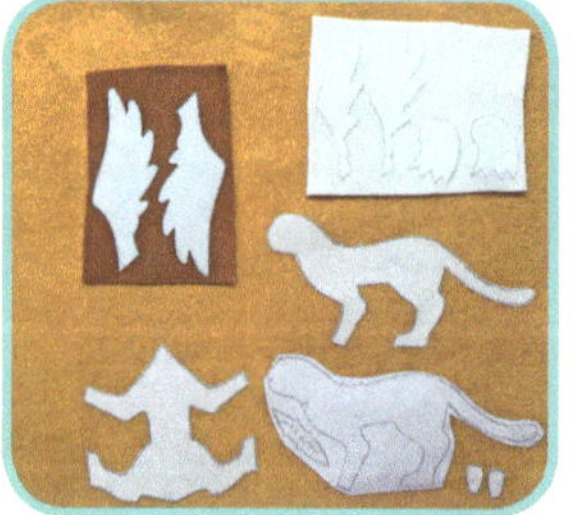

2

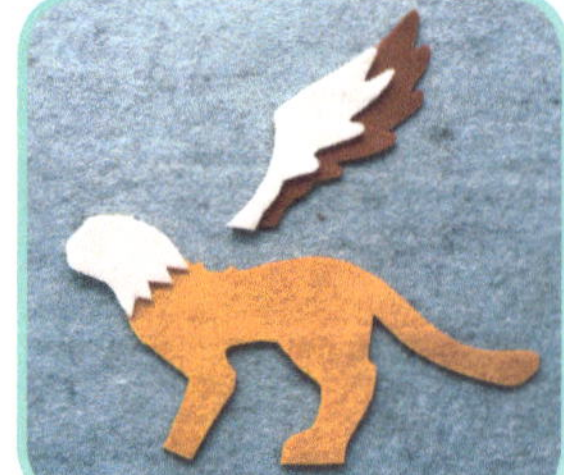

1. Cut out the body pieces, then layer the white head piece onto the body and stitch at neck edge. You may wish to use a drop of fabric glue to keep the white head piece in place as well.

2. Cut out the wing pieces. Lay the white wing over the brown wing pieces and stitch lower edge with a small blanket or whipstitch. Set aside.

To make the Gryphon’s feet:

1

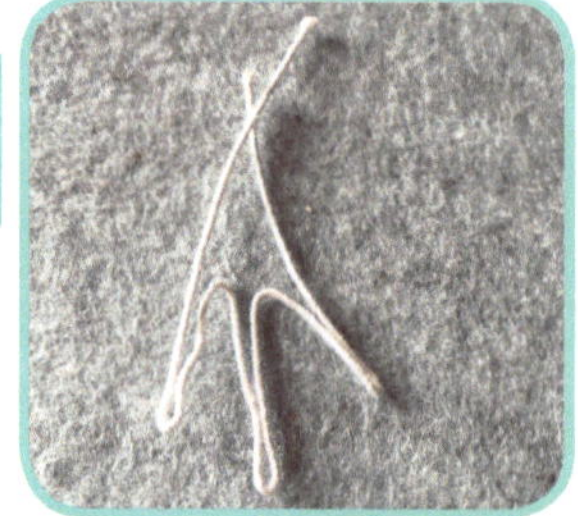

1. Cut floral wire at 8 ½” long. Bend into shape following guide on pattern page 67.

2. Gently unbend. You don’t want to unbend so far that you can’t see where the bends are in the toes.

3. Wrap the wire with three strands of embroidery floss. Wrap past the bend of the first toe about 1/8”. Then press the wires together and continue wrapping up both wires to the second bend on the inside of the foot.

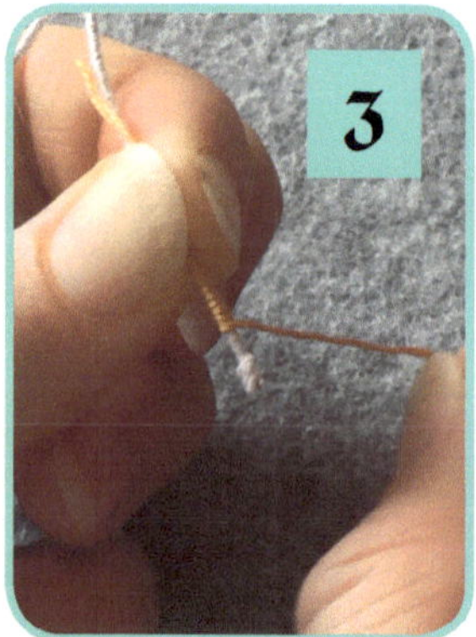

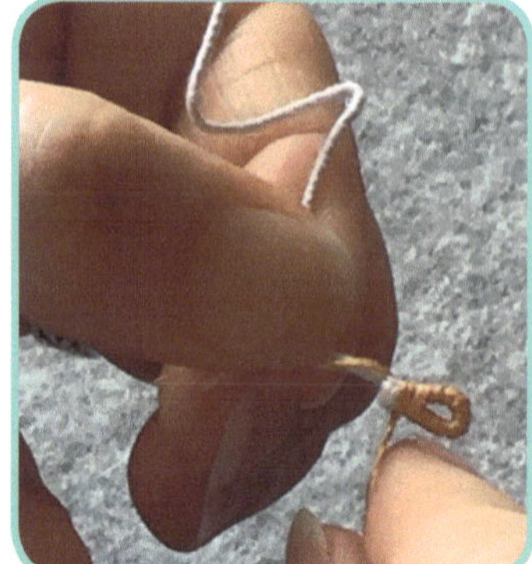

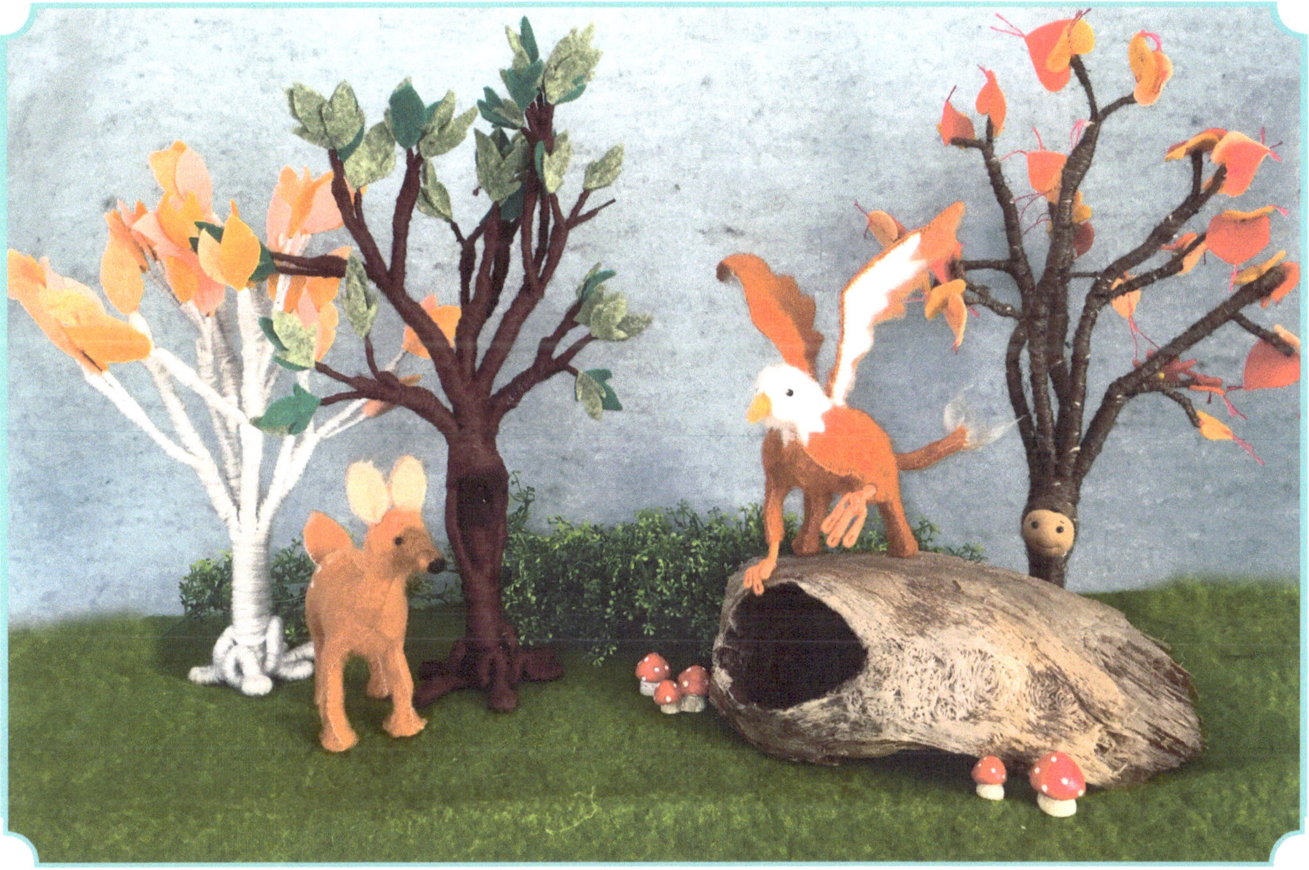

4. Continue wrapping just around the single unwrapped wire until you have wrapped past the second toe about 1/8”.

5. Repeat steps above to finish second and third toes. When you get to the base of the third toe begin wrapping around the whole foot. Don’t forget to wrap in between the toes as well.

6. Continue up the leg. When the whole leg is covered in floss, clip your thread and put a dot of fabric glue to keep your thread from unraveling. Repeat steps for a second foot then set aside to dry.

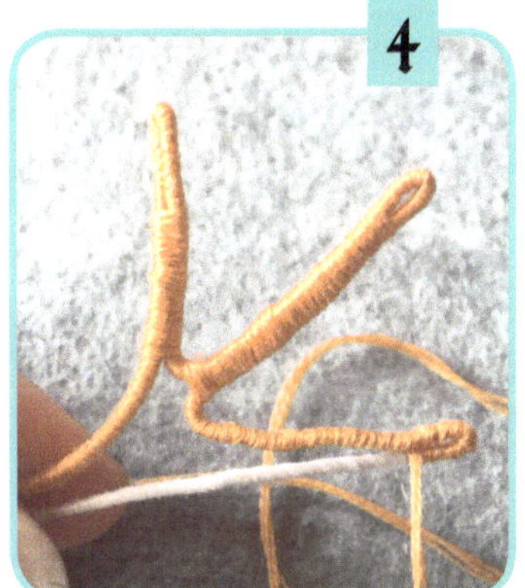

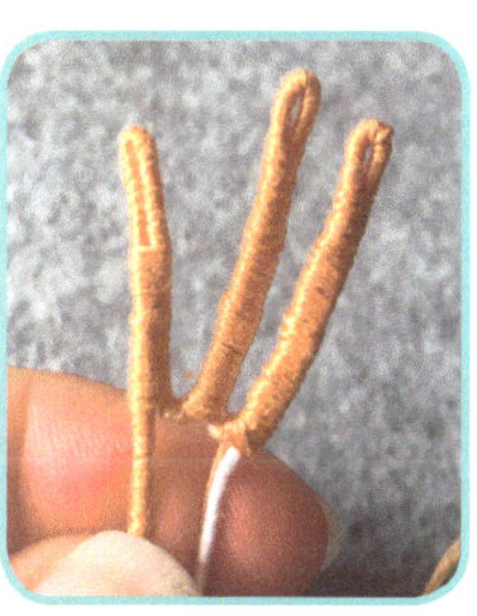

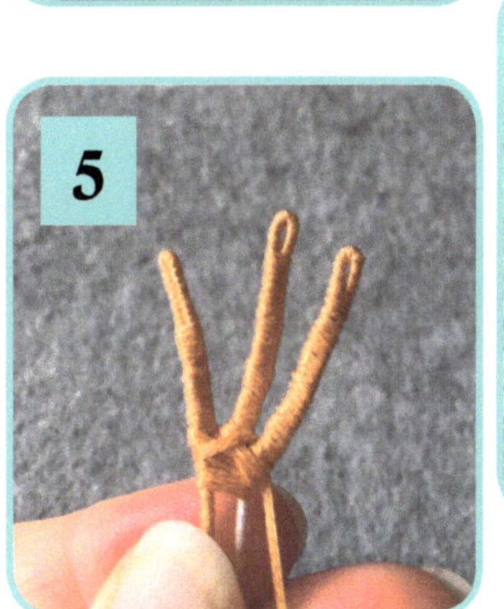

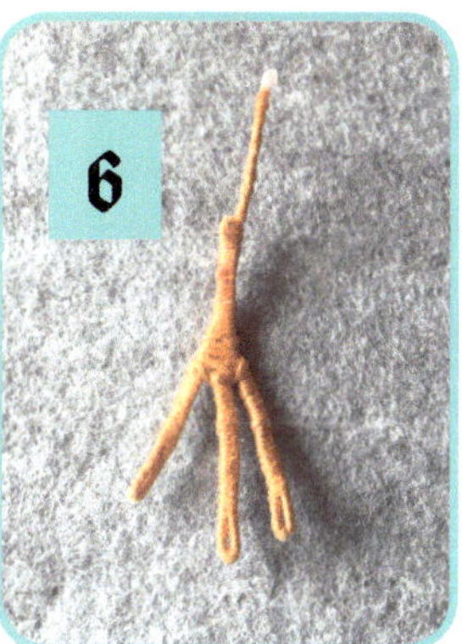

Making the Gryphon Skeleton

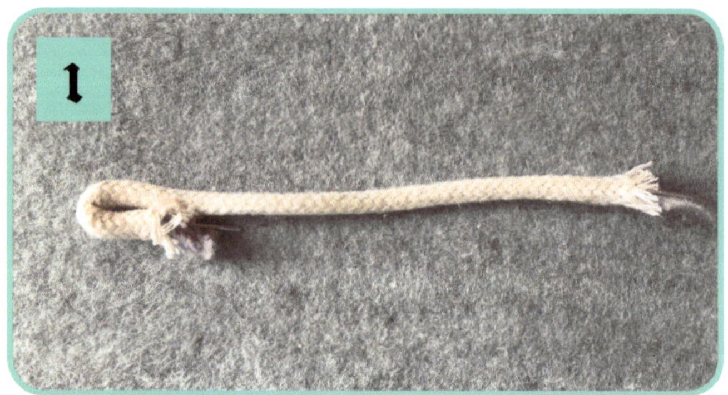

1. To make the gryphon's skeleton start by cutting a piece of figure cord 6 ½" long. Bend one end over an inch.

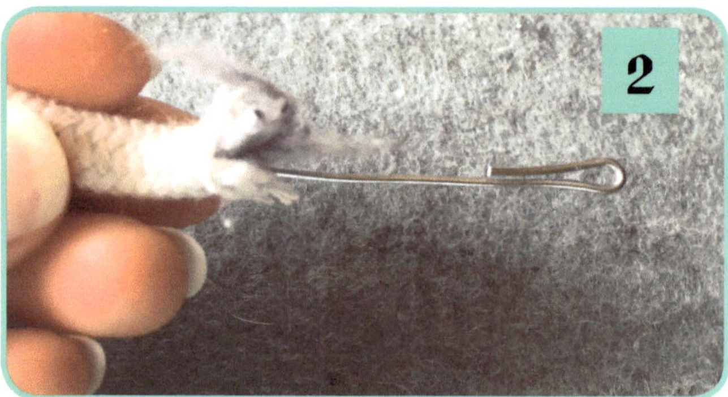

2. Slide back the fabric covering on the tail end. With pliers, bend over the wire. Pull the fabric covering back over the bent end.

3. Cut a piece of chenille stem 4" long and bend one end over half an inch. With your strong cotton thread wrap the unbent end to the tail end of your figure cord — wrap it tight. Then continue wrapping down the tail and wrap the sharp end of the cut wire.

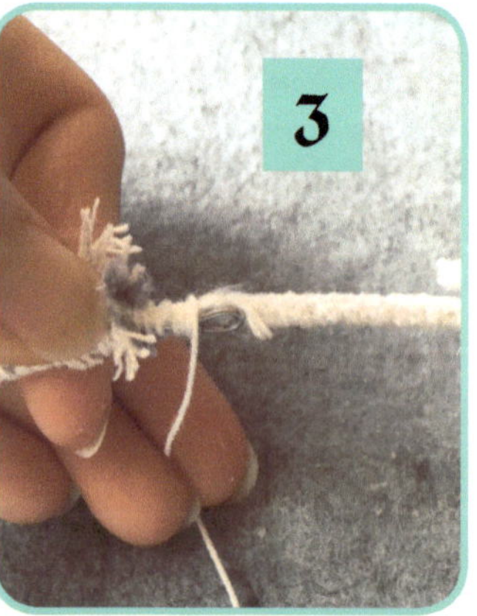

4. Wrap back up the tail toward the head and tie the two ends of cotton thread together.

Wrap the head with your binding thread to cover the sharp point of the wire and tie the two thread ends together.

The photo below shows the tail attached to the spine in step 3.

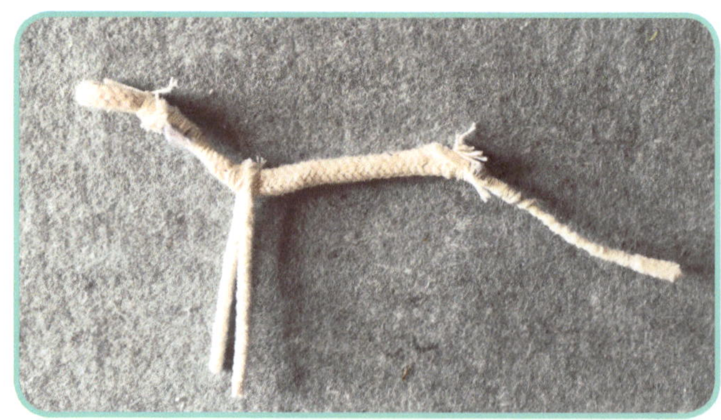

5. Cut a chenille stem for the front legs of the Gryphon. It should be 4 ¾" long. Fold in half and using your pattern as a guide place it over the spine so that it will line up with the front legs. Wrap the joint with binding thread to keep it in place.

★Create the back legs as discussed in the "Make Your Skeleton" section, beginning on page 9, but instead of using figure cord use your chenille stems.

6. To finish the front feet take your wrapped wire foot and join it to your pipe cleaner using the binding thread. Make sure to check the length against your pattern. You want the chenille stem to end just short of the point where the felt on his leg will begin. Make sure you wrap the whole leg so there's no sharp ends sticking out.

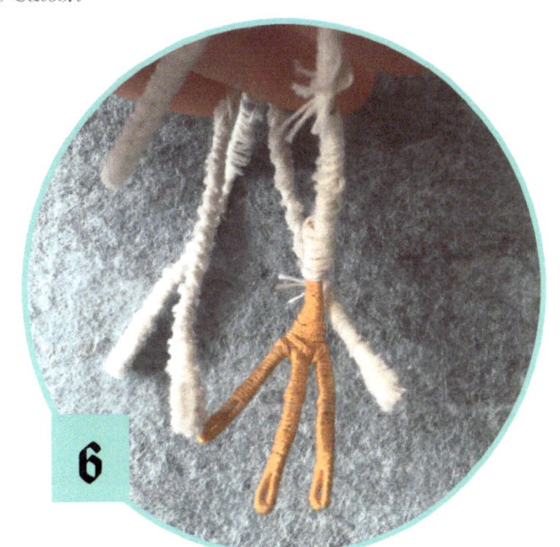

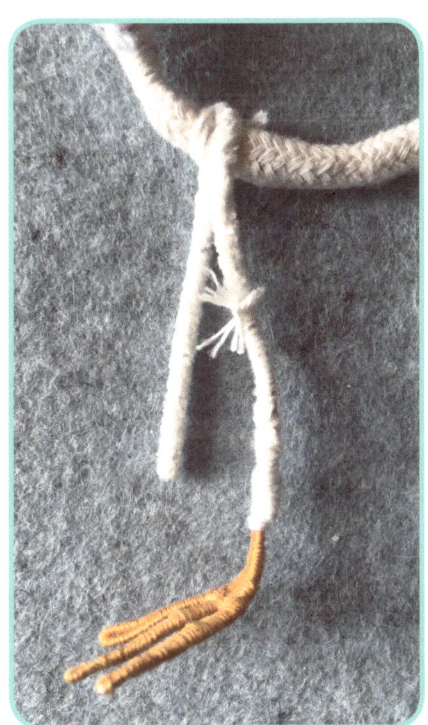

For the wings, follow the same process as for the legs, however, the chenille stems will stick up instead of down and you should anchor the wings behind the front legs as shown in the drawing to the right.

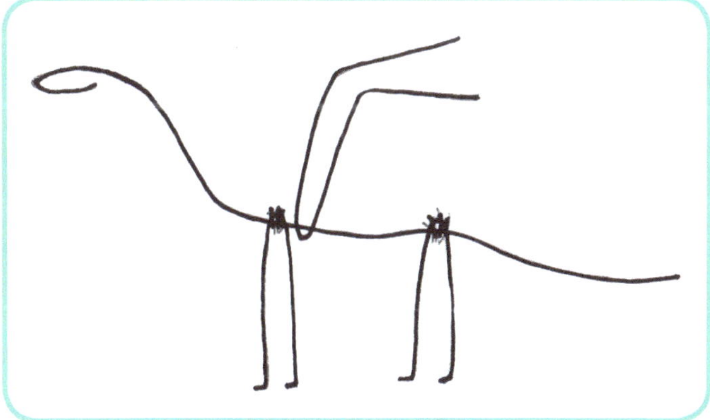

To finish your gryphon, set your skeleton aside, and follow the directions found in the "Making the Felt Body" chapter, beginning on page 11.

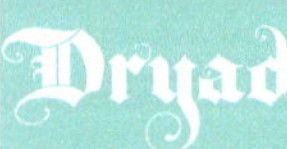

It may look like a tree, but it is a forest spirit. Choose leaf colors of your liking—it is an enchanted forest!

Materials Needed:

- Wool felt in colors of your choice for leaves
- Yarn in your choice of color for trunk
- Scrap of cotton knit
- 48” or more of figure cord
- one or more, 12” cotton plush chenille stems
- Brown, cloth covered floral wire, at least two 8 1/2” long pieces
- Strong thread to match trunk color
- Wool stuffing
- 2 black seed beads (optional)
- Craft glue
- Tools
- Basic sewing supplies (see page 6)

★Note: You could make enchanted trees from these directions without a face as well. Give your tree as many limbs and leaves as you like! Make it shorter, fatter, taller or skinnier. Your imagination is the only limit.

1. Cut five pieces of figure cord at least 12” long.

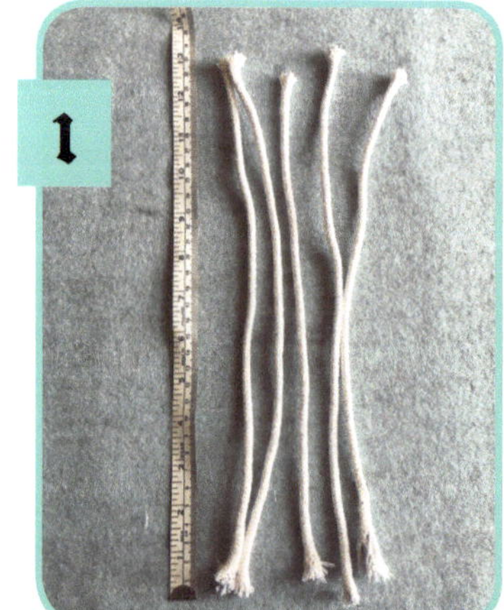

2. Begin wrapping one end of your figure cord about 1- 1/2” from one end. When you get about half an inch from the end, bend your cord and continue wrapping.

3. Wrap the cord about halfway up. Cut your yarn, then anchor the yarn to the figure cord with a fine line of glue. Press and hold for a few seconds. Repeat for the other four lengths of figure cord.

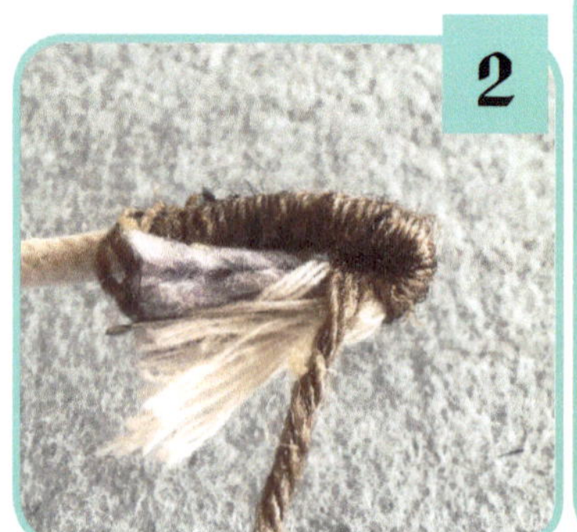

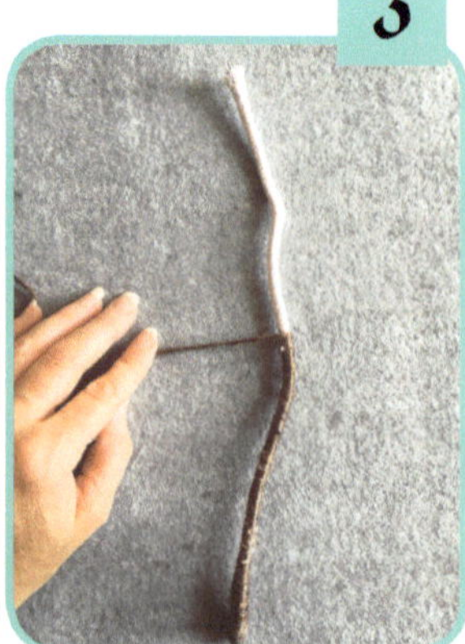

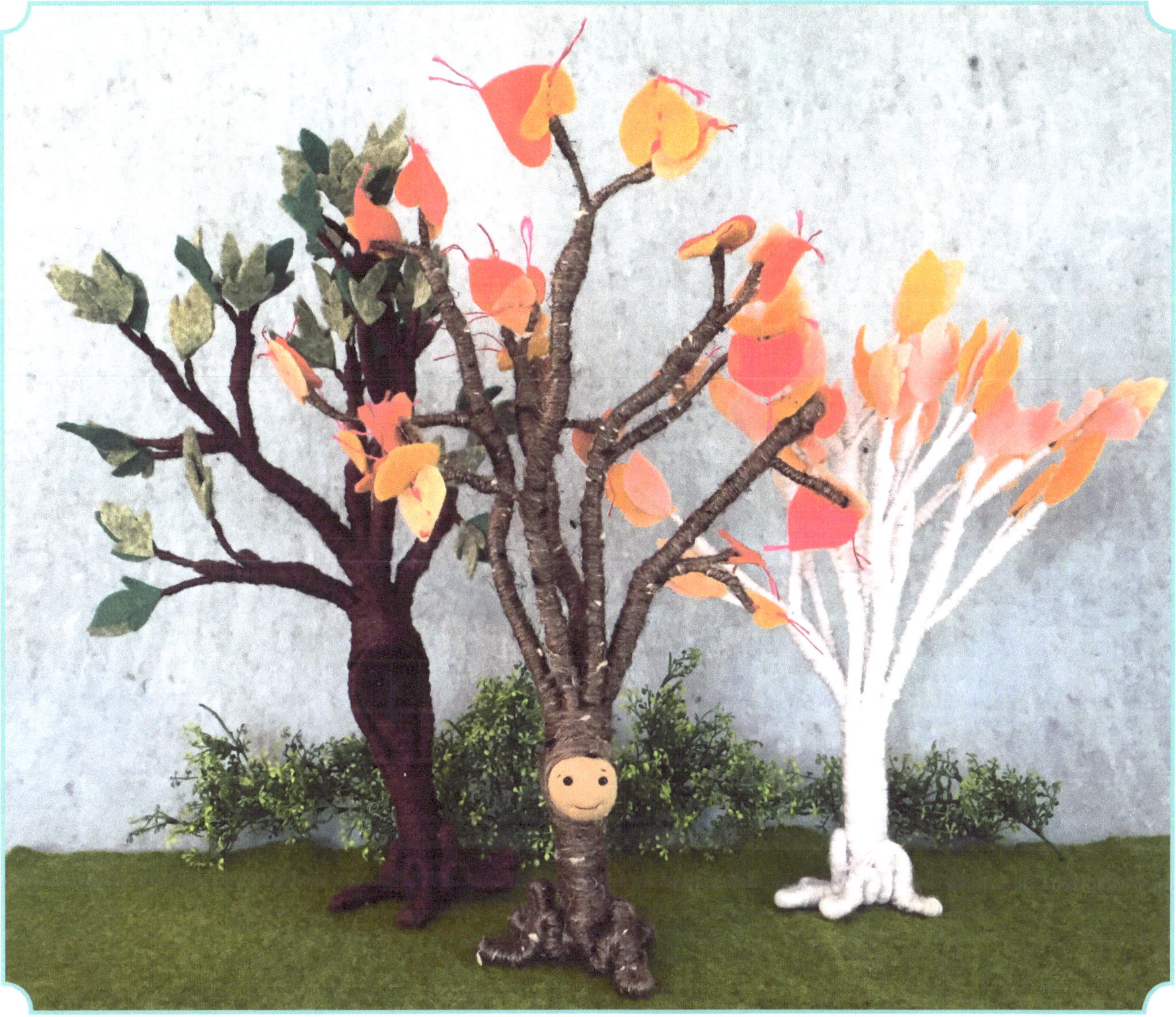

4. Cut a chenille stem in thirds. Cut two lengths of brown floral wire in varying short lengths.

5. Wrap a piece of your floral wire in your yarn just like you did in step 2. Glue the end to stay in place.

6. Now wrap a piece of your chenille stem the same way. When you are about halfway down incorporate the piece of wrapped floral wire and continue wrapping.

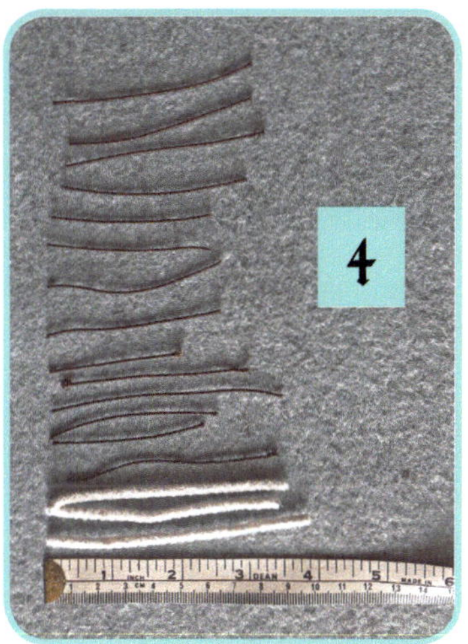

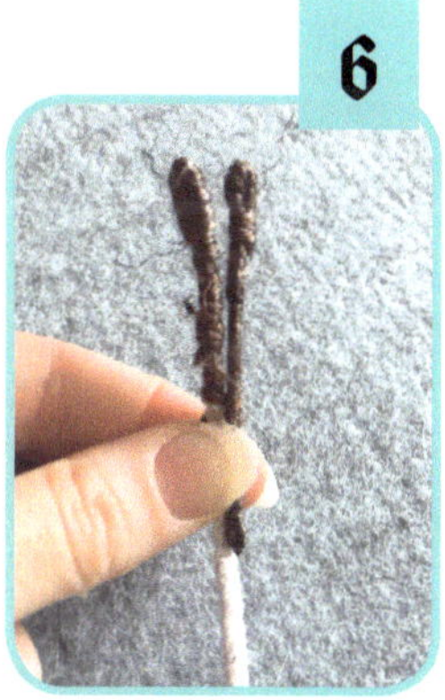

7. Now lay your wrapped limb against the top of the figure cord that is not wrapped and put a few wraps of yarn around it to keep it in place and then glue it. These will be some larger branches coming off the main limbs.

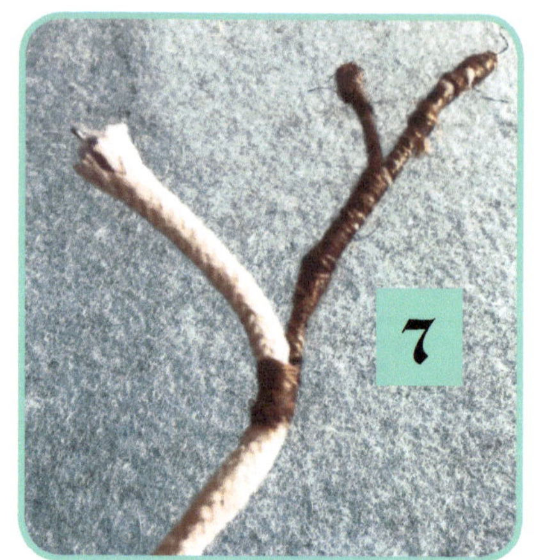

Repeat this process for two other figure cord lengths.

★Note: If you wish to have a thicker trunk, you can add more figure cord lengths.

8. Now wrap the remaining lengths of brown floral wire and incorporate them into your figure cord lengths in groups of twos and threes. These are smaller branches coming off the main limbs. Don't forget to add branches to the top of your limb too!

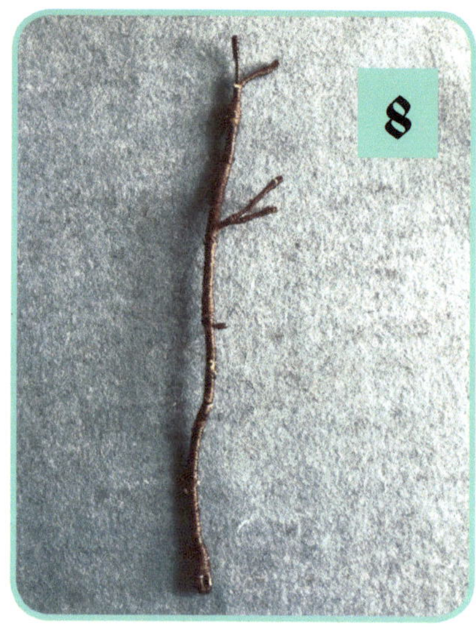

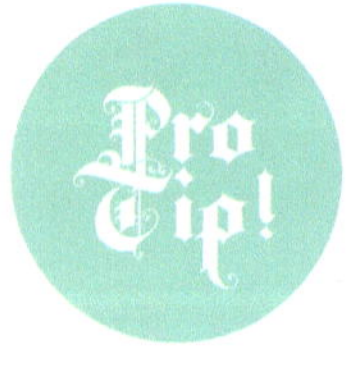

Pro tip: you can beef up the width of your branch by wrapping your figure cord loosely down and then back up and then wrapping more tightly back down the limb toward the "trunk".

9. To make the dryads face, cut a circle out of cotton knit in a similar color to your tree yarn. The circle should be about 2- 1/2 inches across. Gather the circle about a quarter of an inch from the edge with some strong thread in a color that is close to your tree bark.

10. Pull your gathers a little bit and stuff your circle with wool stuffing. Continue to pull your gathers and stuff your circle until you're satisfied with the shape. Knot your thread.

11. Decide which edge of your head is the top and which is the bottom. Sculpt your face lightly with your thread. You want to make two indents for the eyes and two indents for the corners of the mouth.

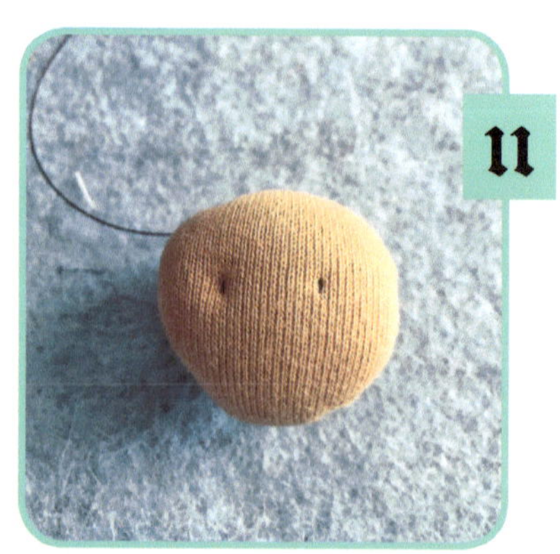

12. With your threaded needle go back into one corner of the mouth and pull the string across to the other corner of the mouth. Knot the thread in the back of the head. Now you can embroider your eyes or you can use seed beads for a more reflective eye. Set head aside.

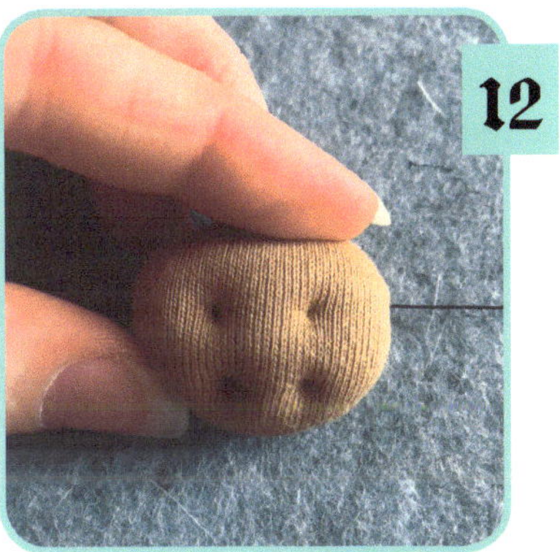

13. Wrap three of your figure cord limbs together near the middle. Don't cut your yarn, but push it in between two limbs to keep it from unraveling while sewing the face on. Using a ladder stitch, sew the head to your three connected branches.

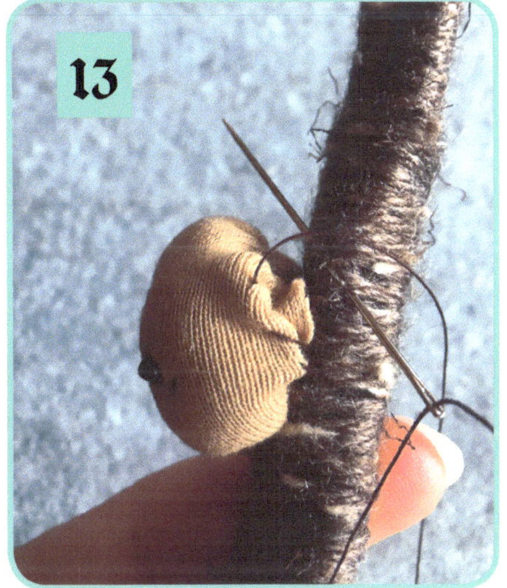

14. Put the other two limbs on each side of the face—one on each side.

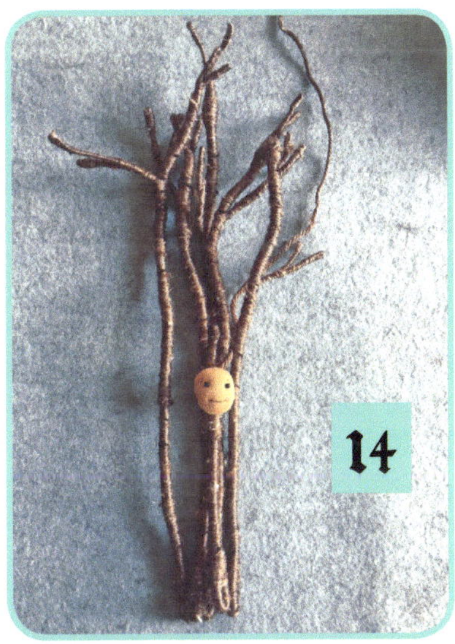

15. Continue wrapping the tree trunk with the yarn above and below the head and crossing on each side.

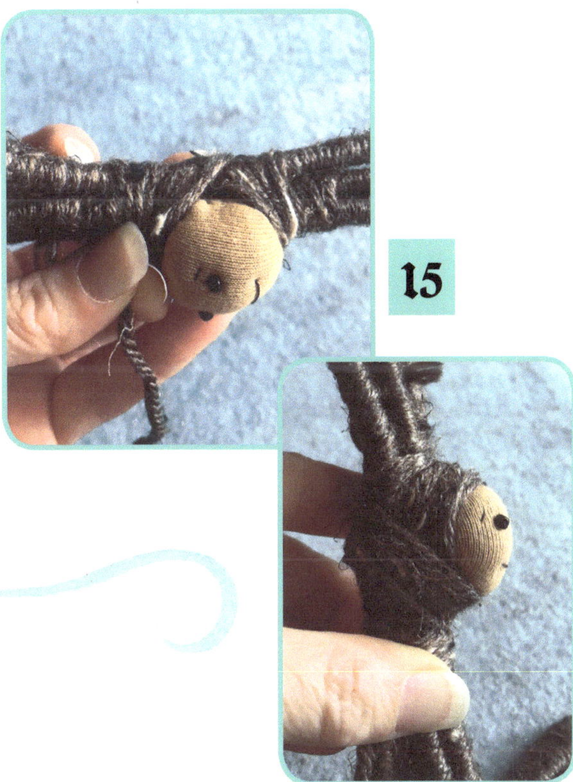

16. When the head is completely wrapped, bend the "feet" of the dryad so it looks like her legs are tucked. Make sure she can stand on her own. Wrap the yarn down the trunk and in between her "legs" to keep them in place. When the trunk is wrapped successfully wrap the yarn back up above the head.

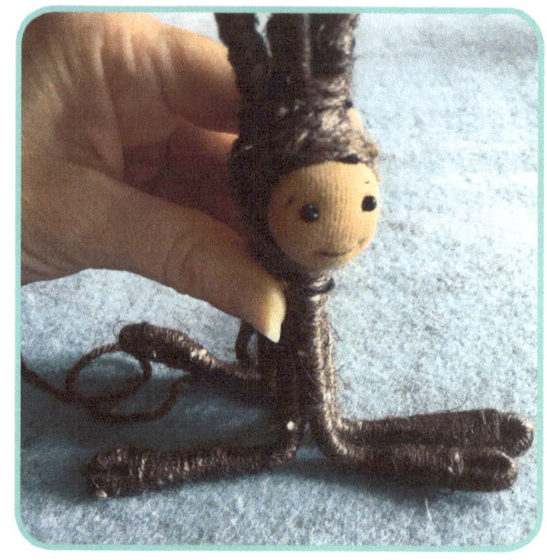

16

17. Thread your yarn onto a yarn needle, make a knot at the back of the trunk and bury the end and clip yarn.

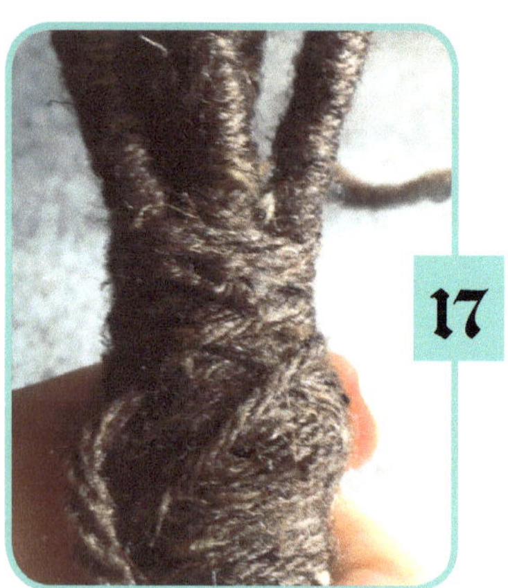

17

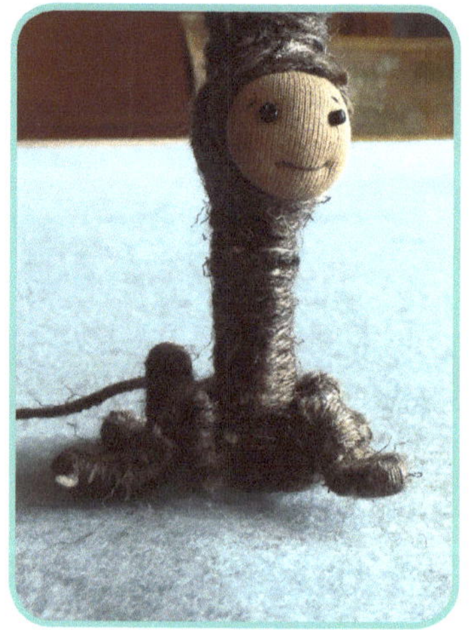

18. Cut leaf shapes from wool felt. You'll want at least two leaves per branch end. With embroidery floss, stitch the leaves to the end of each branch.

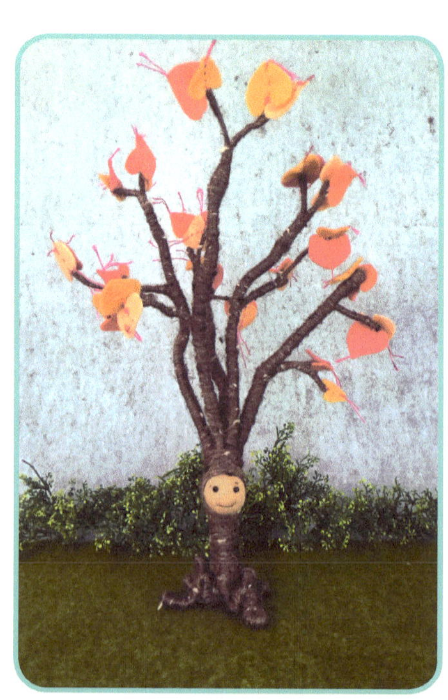

☆Try these leaf shapes! or one of your own.

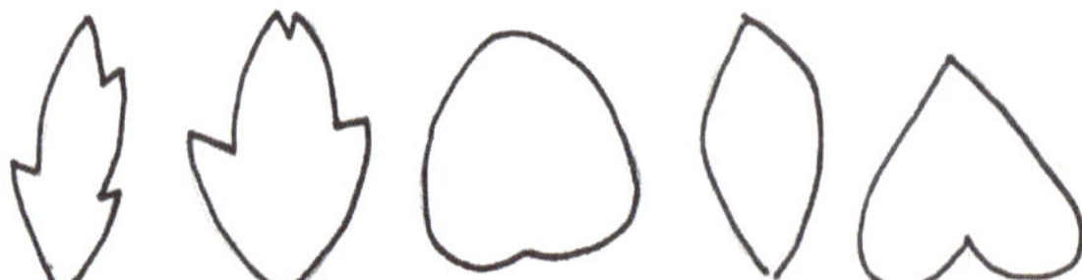

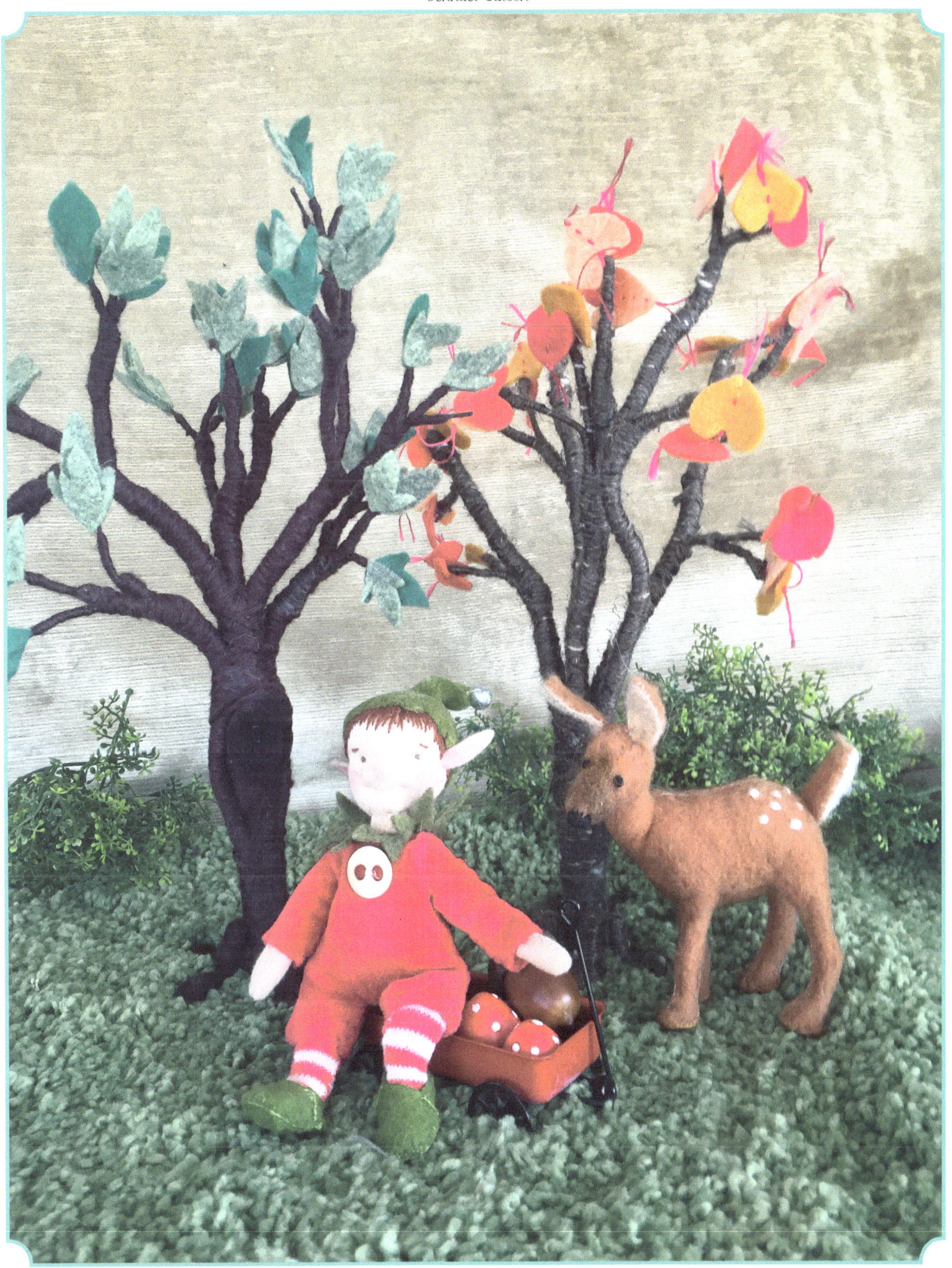

Picking toadstools in the Enchanted Forest is tiring. I need a break!

Gnome

A cute, bearded little dude who has a bendy doll base which makes him a quick and easy project.

Materials Needed:

- 4" tall bendy doll base
- 2 fat quarters of cotton plush velour fabric— for pants, shirt, and hood
- 4" of 7/8" wide cotton gauze tubing for inner head
- 4" x 3" rectangle of cotton interlock knit
- 2 —10mm wool balls for hands
- 1— 5mm wool felt bead for nose
- Scrap of brown wool for belt
- Assorted embroidery floss colors to match plush velor fabric and color for eyes
- Genziana wool thread for hair, beard, and eyebrows
- Binding thread
- Wool stuffing
- Tools
- Basic sewing supplies (see page 6)
- **Optional materials**: two tiny buttons, ribbon for scarf, metallic embroidery floss for belt buckle

☆Note: It would be easy to make female gnomes too! Just add some length to the shirt and call it a dress!

1. Cut a 4" length of your cotton gauze tubing. Stitch one of the short ends closed then turn right side out (RSO).

2. Cut a 3" wide by 4 -1/2" long piece of cotton knit. Make sure the stretch goes across the width.

3. Fold the cotton knit in half so that it is 1-1/2" wide. With a quarter inch seam allowance sew down the long end of the cotton knit. Trim the seam allowance until it is only an eighth of an inch wide. Turn RSO.

4. With your wool roving wrap a ball that is 4" in diameter. Slip your ball into your stockinette tube.

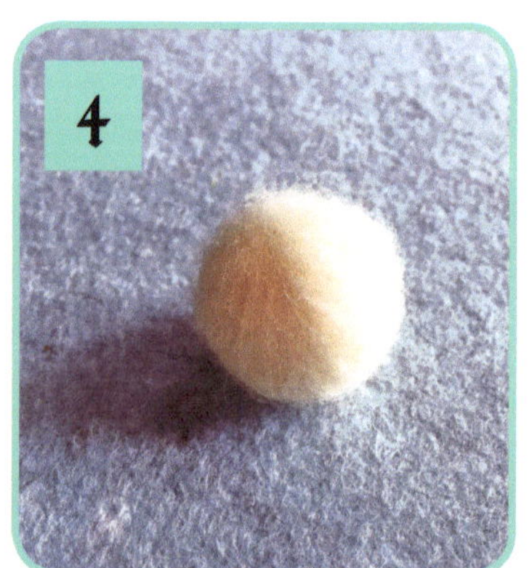

Pro Tip!

Pro tip: If you want to make a nice firm head, you can felt the ball with a felting needle. Don't make it too firm though, or you won't be able to pull the head down enough to sit on the wooden neck properly.

5. Now slip the tube over your wooden bendy doll body. Pull it down pretty tightly making sure that the wooden neck piece is in the center of your ball and with scissors, snip the gauze tubing just above the wire arm.

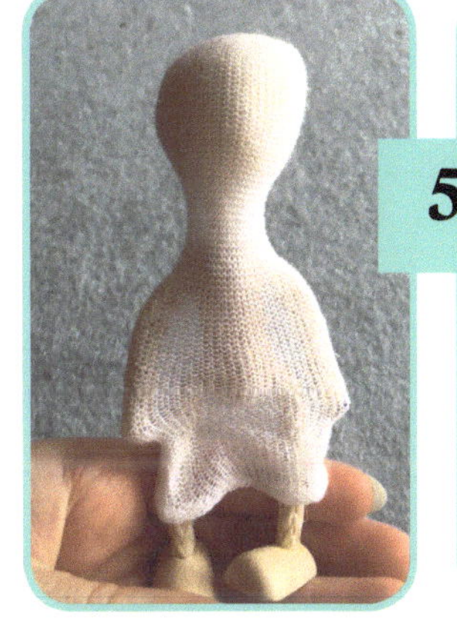

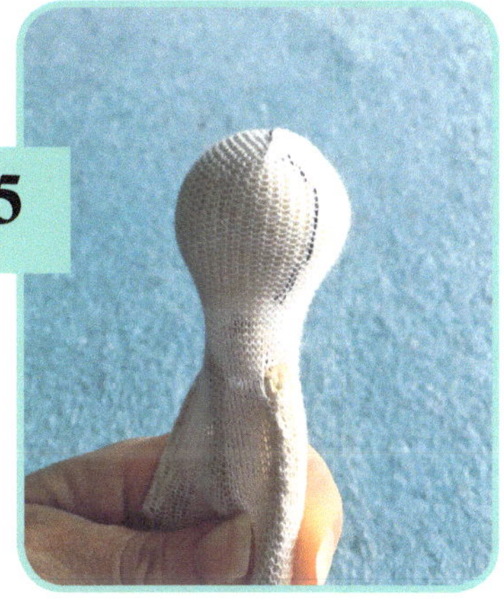

6. Push your arm wires through the little holes you just made. More than likely you will have to take the head back off to do this. Now with some strong thread and pulling down on gauze rather firmly, tie off the head.

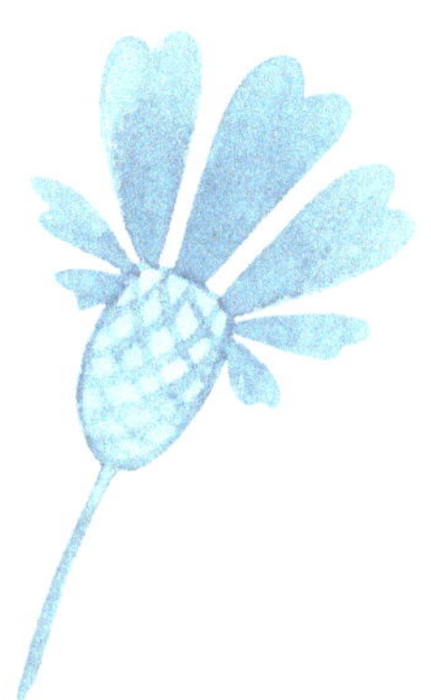

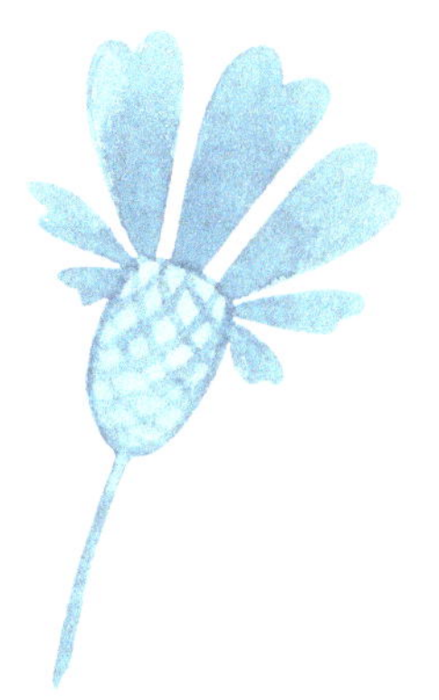

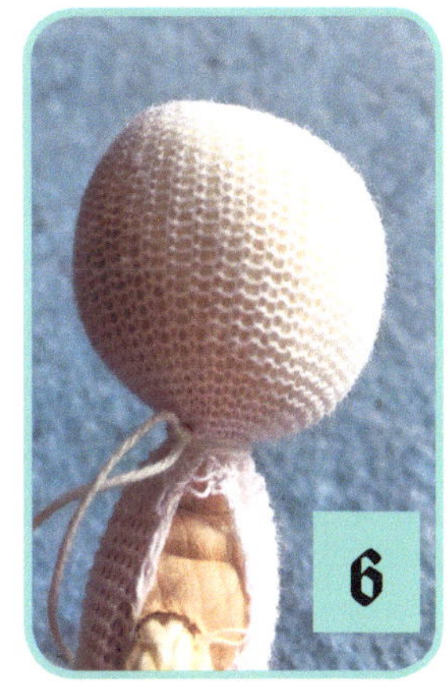

Below is the head with both the vertical and horizontal strings tied around head.

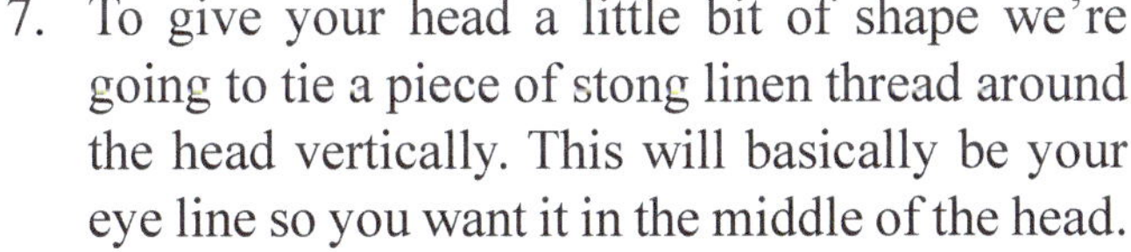

7. To give your head a little bit of shape we're going to tie a piece of stong linen thread around the head vertically. This will basically be your eye line so you want it in the middle of the head.

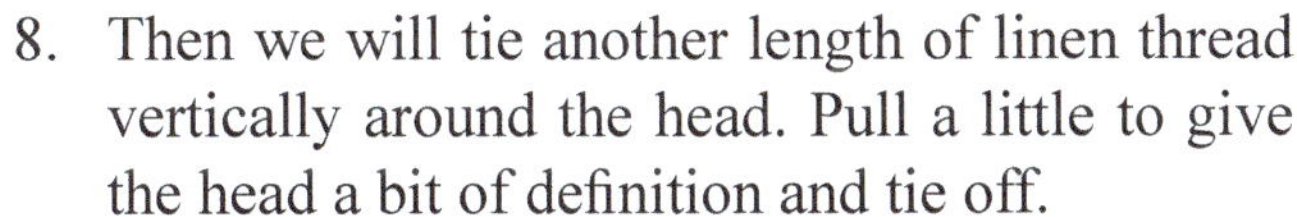

8. Then we will tie another length of linen thread vertically around the head. Pull a little to give the head a bit of definition and tie off.

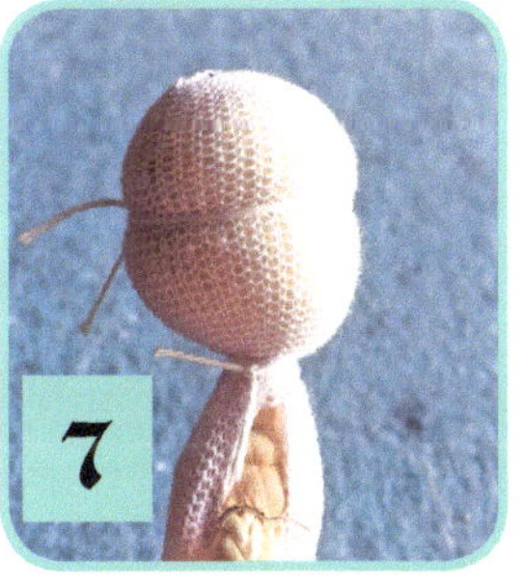

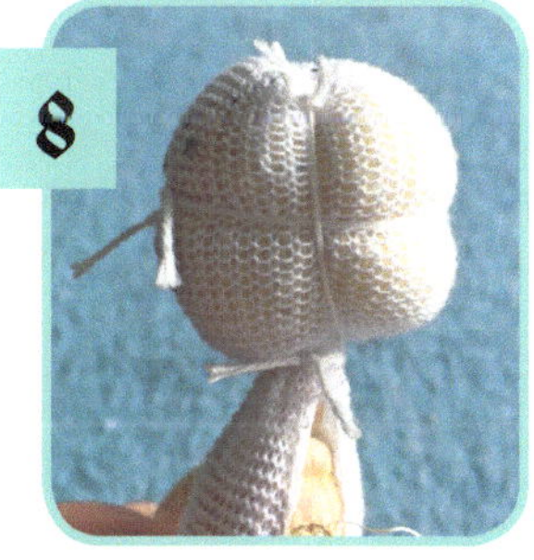

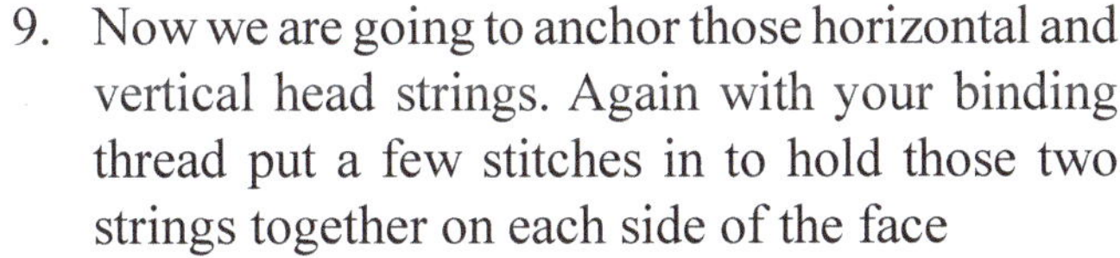

9. Now we are going to anchor those horizontal and vertical head strings. Again with your binding thread put a few stitches in to hold those two strings together on each side of the face

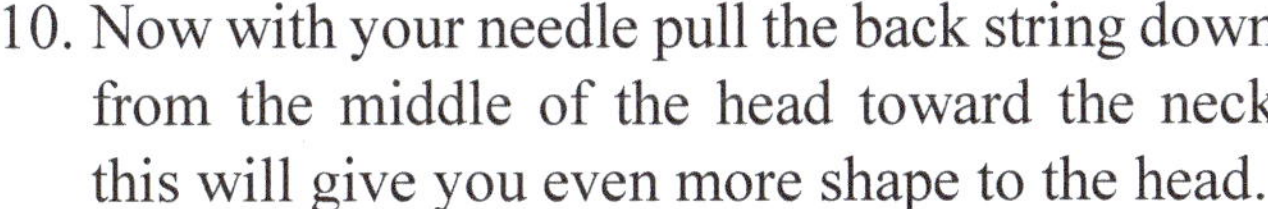

10. Now with your needle pull the back string down from the middle of the head toward the neck this will give you even more shape to the head.

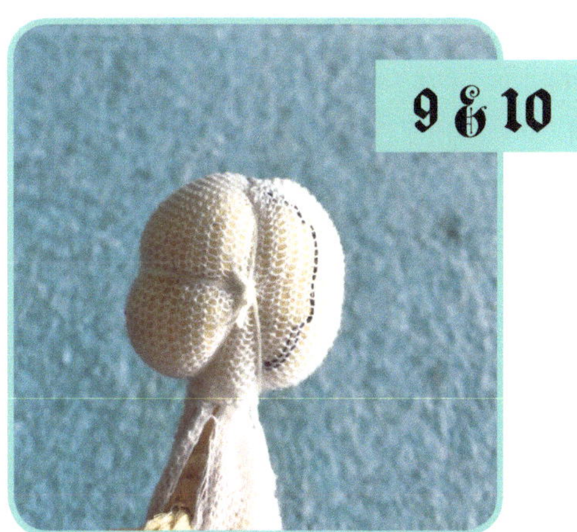

11. Stitch the string you just pulled down from the back of the head to the string from front of the head with a little bit of a zigzag stitch. Knot your thread when you reach the anchor knot at the side of face.

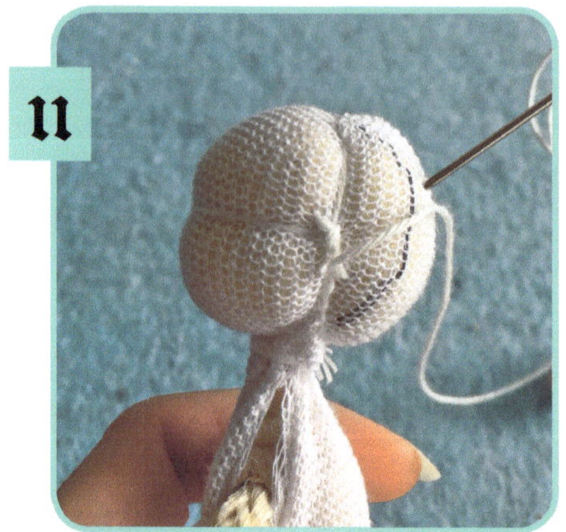

12. Just under the horizontal eye line thread sew on your 5mm wool bead for a nose. Or you may wish to embroider the nose on later.

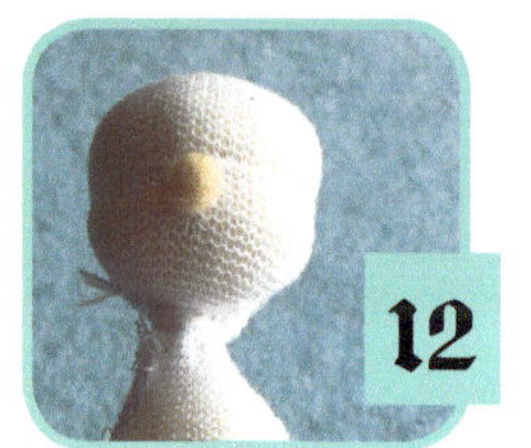

13. Now stuff some wool in his belly to give him a bit of a well fed look.

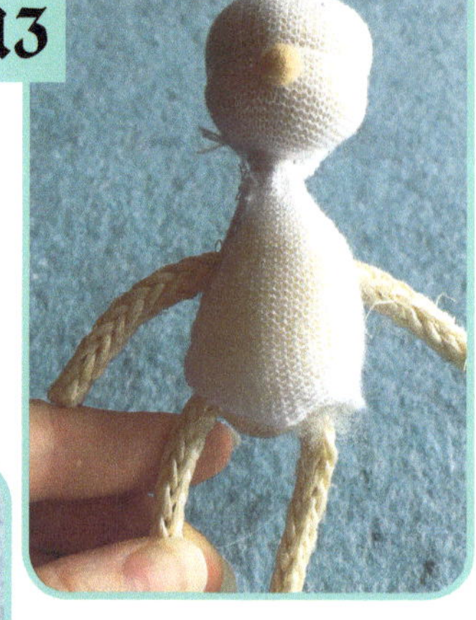

14. Stitch the bottom of the gauze closed between his legs.

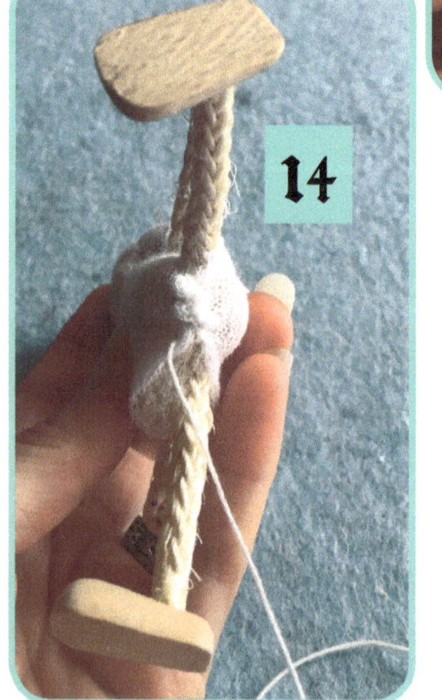

15. Sew the 10mm wool balls onto the end of his arms for his hands.

16. With the seam in the back of the head, pull the cotton knit over your gnome's head. It's going to be a little bit like stuffing a sausage!

17. When you have the skin over his head tie it tight under his head (around) his neck with your binding thread. Then snip two holes on each side by his shoulders and put his arms and hands through. Now sew the bottom between his legs.

18. Cut the fabric left at the top of the head in three places. Lay them on top of each other and sew them down with the floss color that you want for his eyes. Knot your thread but don't cut it.

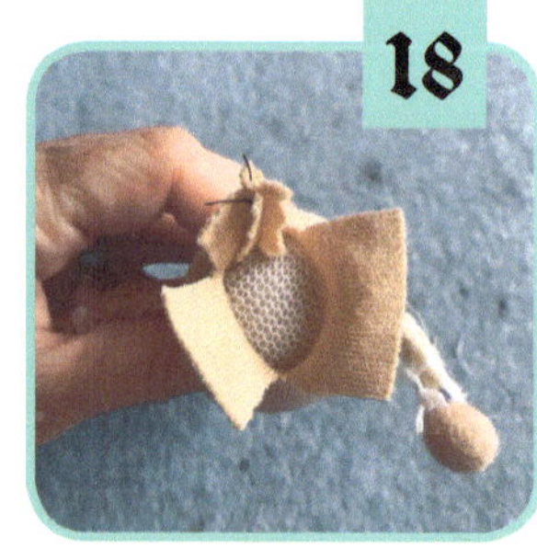

19. Place two small pins where you want to embroider his eyes and check placement. When you are happy with placement, use your threaded needle to make two indents for the eyes, pull gently and knot the string in the back of his head.

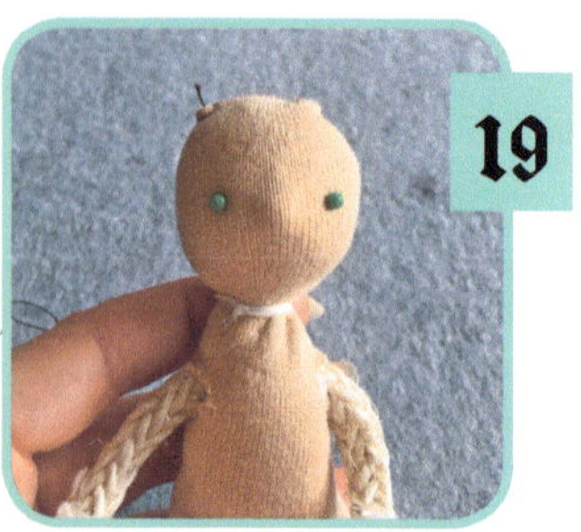

20. Now embroider eyes using three strands of embroidery floss. Insert your needle through the back of the head leaving a three inch tail. Stitch your eye (following diagram) and then exit needle out back of head close to thread tail. Tie the two thread ends together.

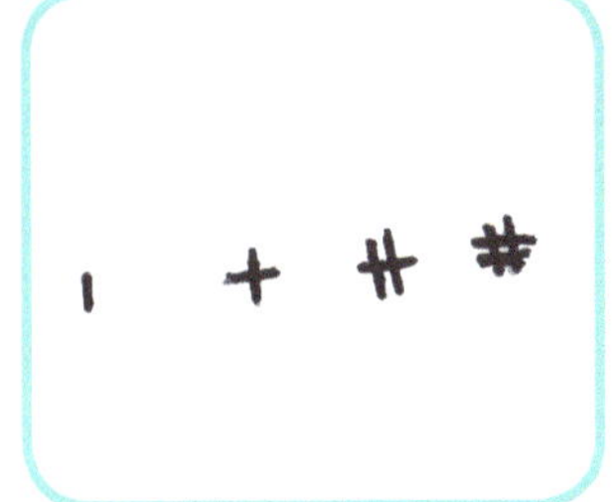

You can also use a french knot to embroider your gnome's eyes.

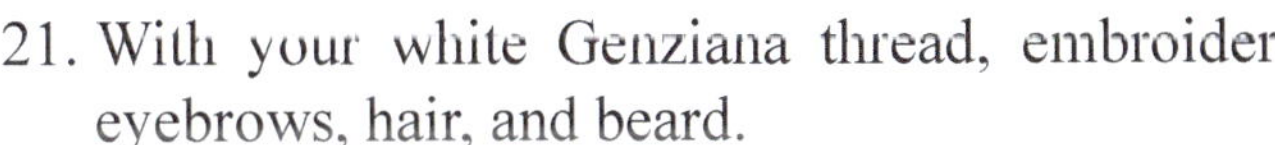

21. With your white Genziana thread, embroider eyebrows, hair, and beard.

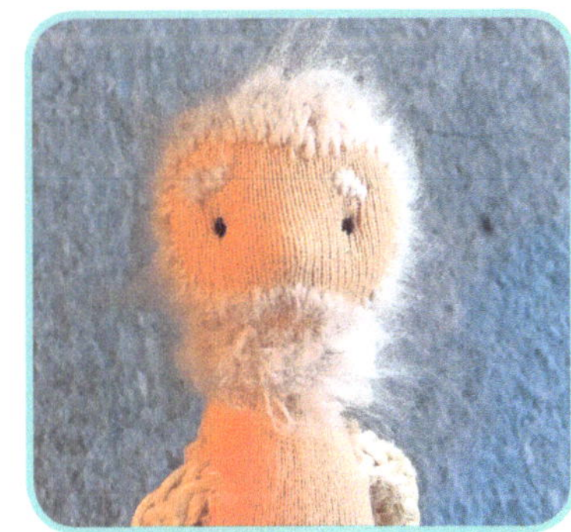

21

Your gnome can have a short or long beard. To make a longer beard, don't pull your thread tight to skin, but leave little loops. To make your beard, hair, and eyebrows fuzzy, gently brush it with a bunka brush.

22. Cut pants, shirt, and hood pieces out of cotton velvet. Sew pants with RST at side seams and inseam. Turn RSO and slip onto Gnome. Gather waist and knot thread. Clip ends of thread.

23. With RST sew hat from point to neck edge. Knot thread and clip ends.

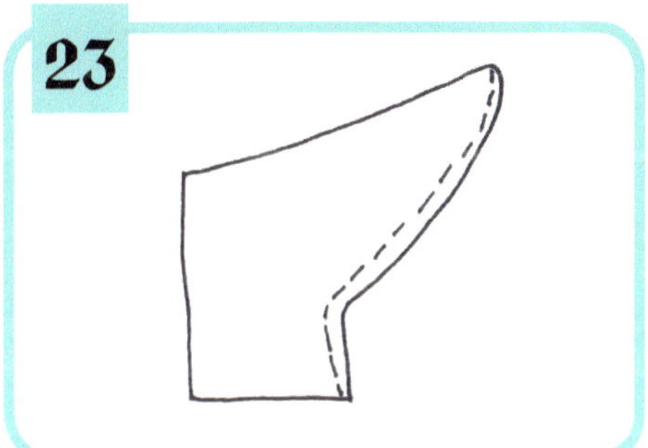

24. Put hat on gnome head. Roll edge under a bit and pin to keep in place. With two strands of floss and a tiny ladder stitch, sew edge of hood to head. Knot and bury thread, clip end.

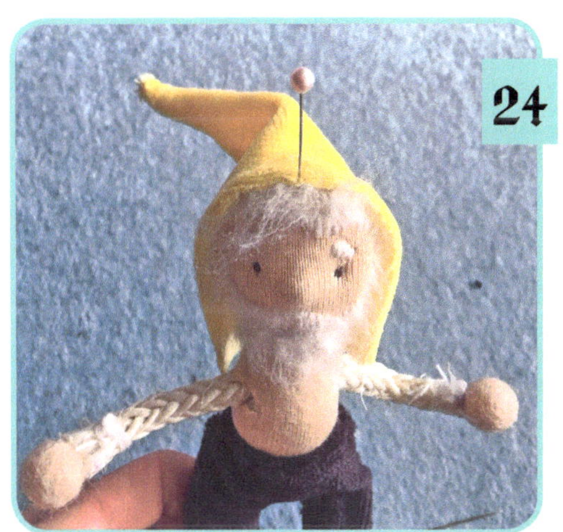

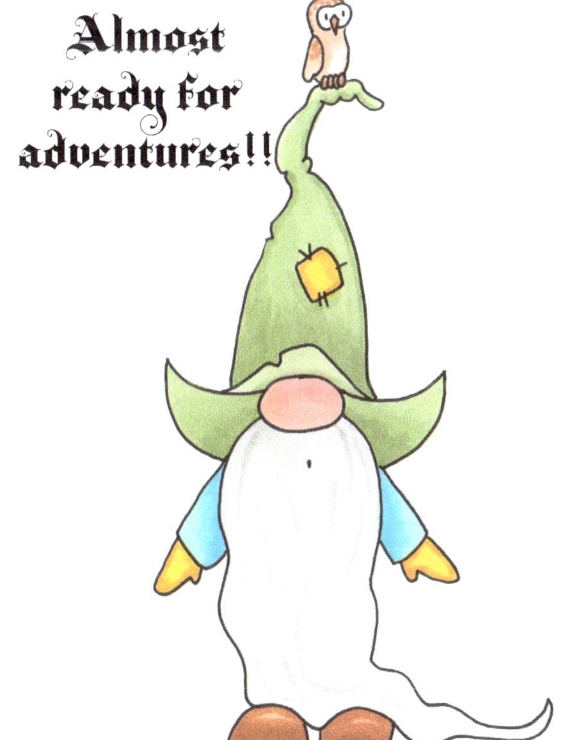

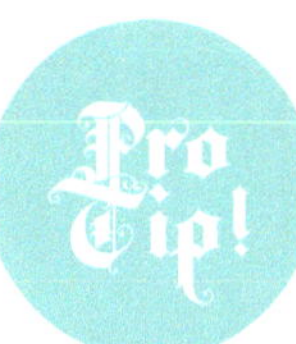

Pro-Tip: You can also embroider hair all over your Gnome's head and give him a removeable hat made from felt instead of sewing on the hood.

25. With RST sew shirt starting with the top sleeve seam. Next sew the underarm seams. Turn RSO and slip onto gnome.

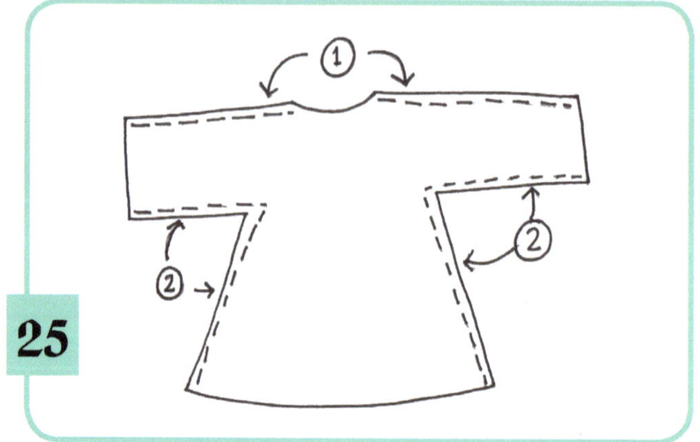

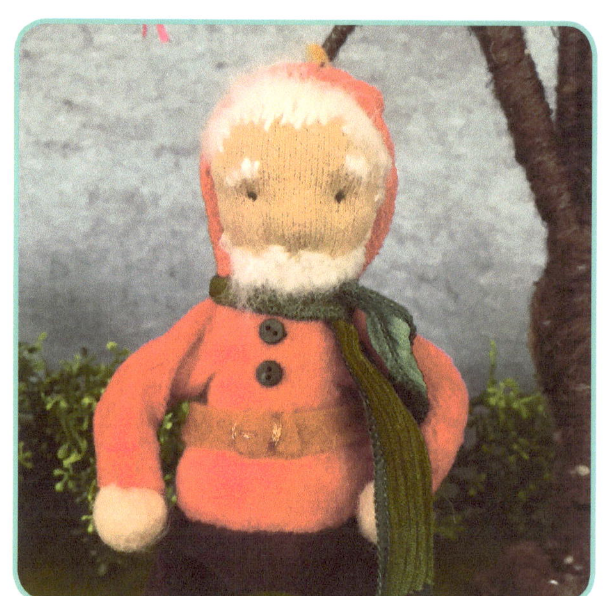

26. Roll bottom edge of shirt under and stitch to pants with a tiny ladder stitch.

27. Roll hem of sleeve and stitch to hand with a tiny ladder stitch.

28. Push bottom edge of hood under neck edge of shirt. Gather edge of neck and then ladder stitch hood to neck edge of shirt.

29. Sew two tiny buttons onto shirt if desired.

30. Cut a narrow piece of felt as a belt. Wrap around Gnome tummy. Embroider belt buckle with two strands of metallic thread.

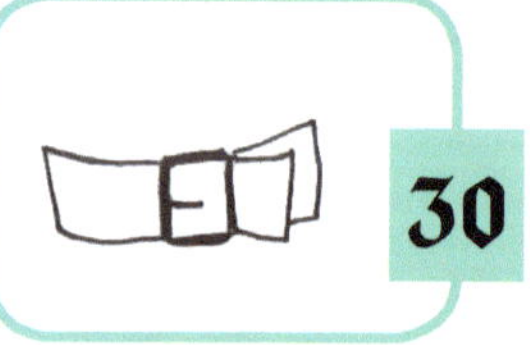

31. If it's a bit chilly, tie a ribbon scarf on your gnome friend. You can use a bit of fray check, fabic glue, or clear nail polish to keep the ends from fraying.

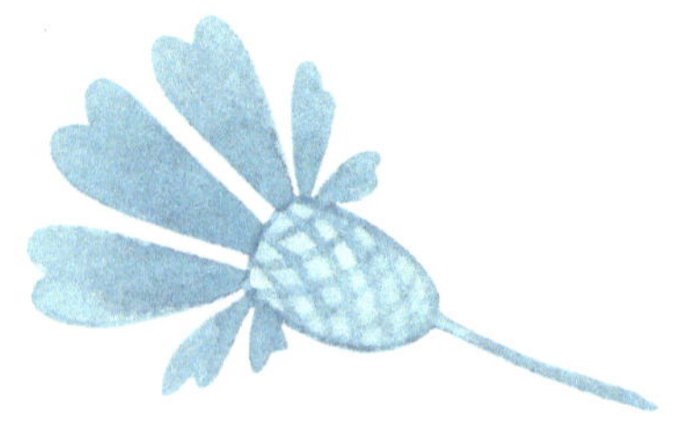

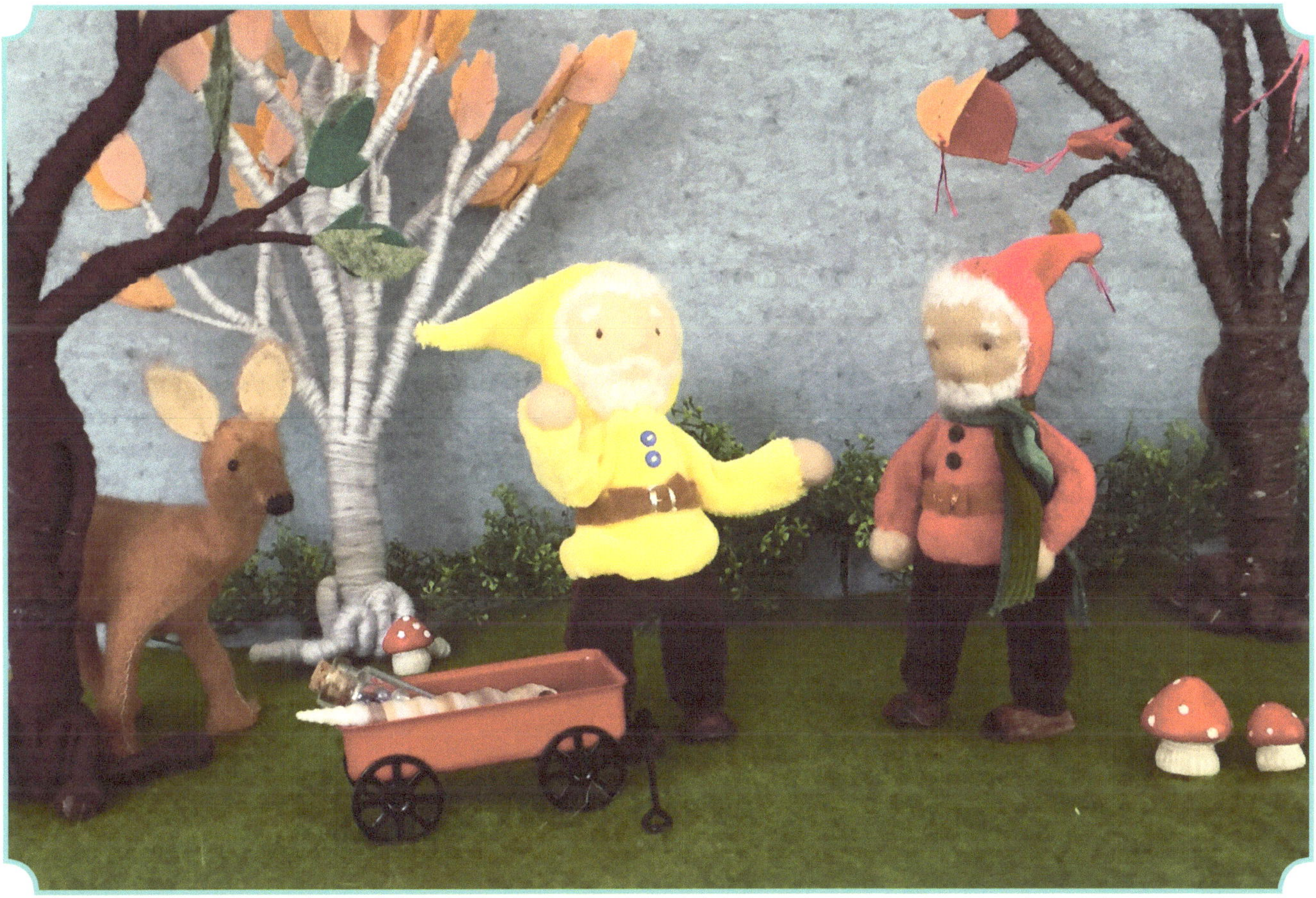

What adventures will your Gnome have?

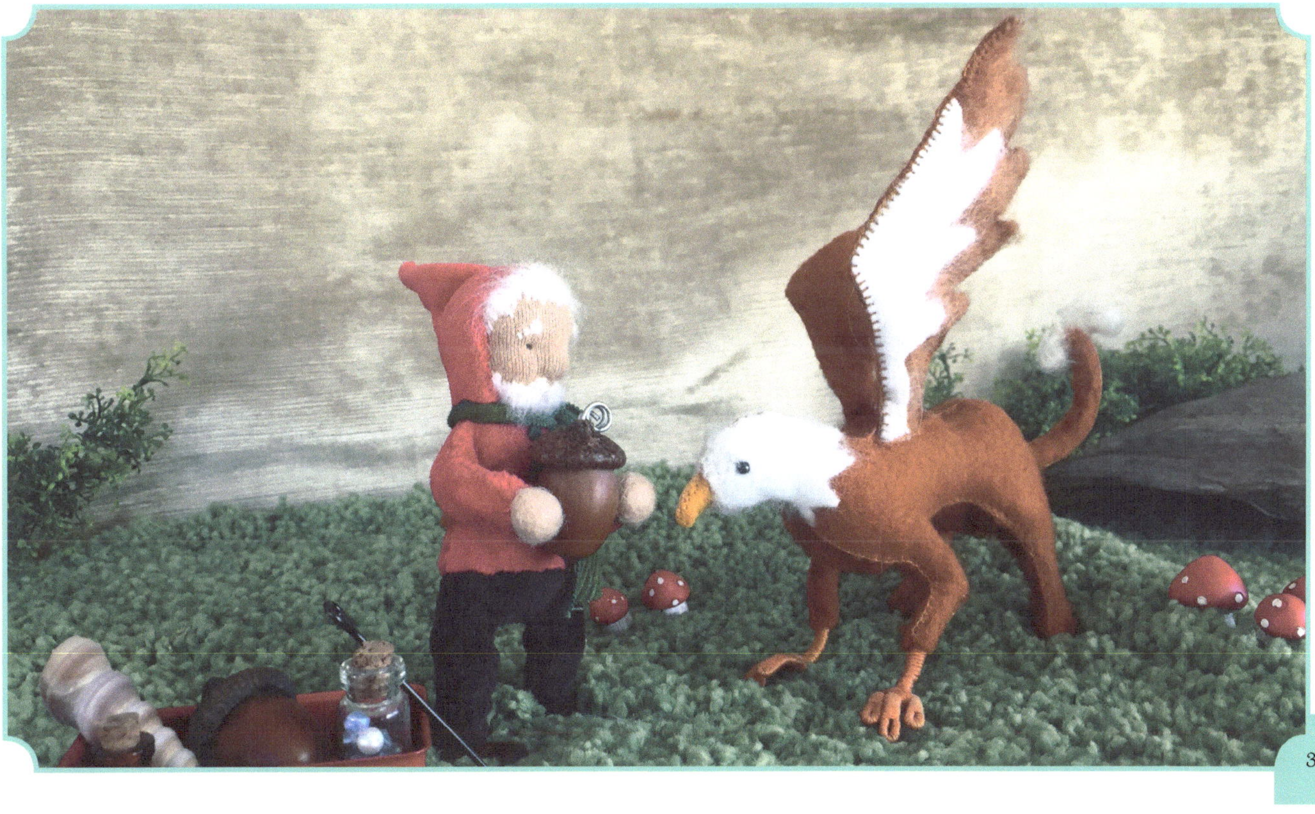

Knight

Whether it's slaying dragons or rescuing priceless treasures, a knight is always ready for adventure!

Materials Needed:

- 4" tall bendy doll base
- 3" x 6" rectangle of glitter or metallic felt
- 8" x 12" sheet of felt in black for undershirt and collar
- 8" x 12" sheet of felt for pants and helmet in gray
- 6" square of felt for shoes
- 4" of 7/8" wide cotton gauze tubing for inner head
- 4" x 3" cotton interlock knit
- 2 —10mm wool balls for hands
- 1— 5mm wool felt bead for nose
- Assorted embroidery floss colors to match wool felt and color for eyes and hair
- Binding thread
- Wool stuffing
- Tools
- Basic sewing supplies (see page 6)
- **Optional materials**: scrap of wool felt for shield on back of armour

★Note: Can't find metallic felt? You can add a bit of sparkle to your knight's armour using metallic floss and a chain stitch. Embroider lines down the wool felt before sewing the armor pieces together.

The knight is made the same way as the Gnome. Follow the directions starting on page 30 to make the basic body. Add as much or as little facial hair as you want and give your knight a bit of a smile with some pink floss. The directions for his clothes are as follows:

1. Cut two sleeves out of black felt. Wrap the sleeve around his arm so that the edges meet in the back. Whipstitch or blanket stitch the edges together with matching floss.

2. Cut out two undershirt pieces from black felt. Sew the front to the back at shoulder seam using a small blanket stitch.

3. At the side seams, pull the front side flap of the undershirt (under the arms) over the

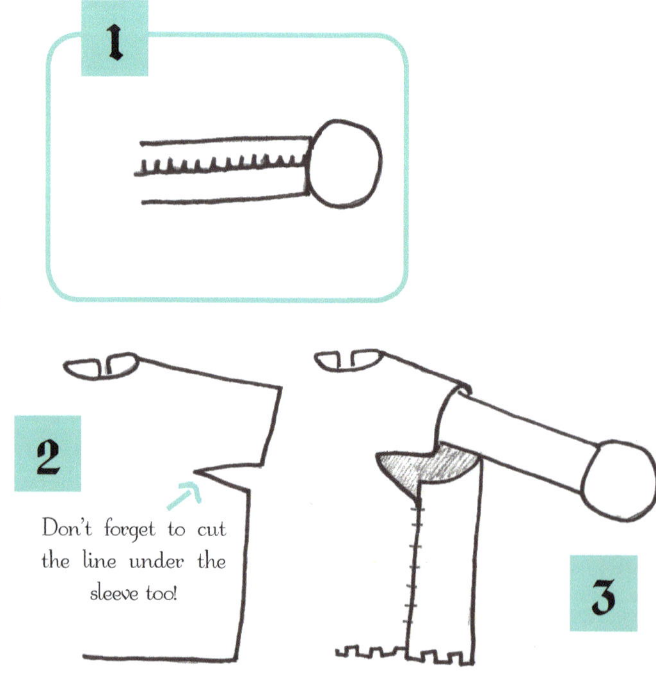

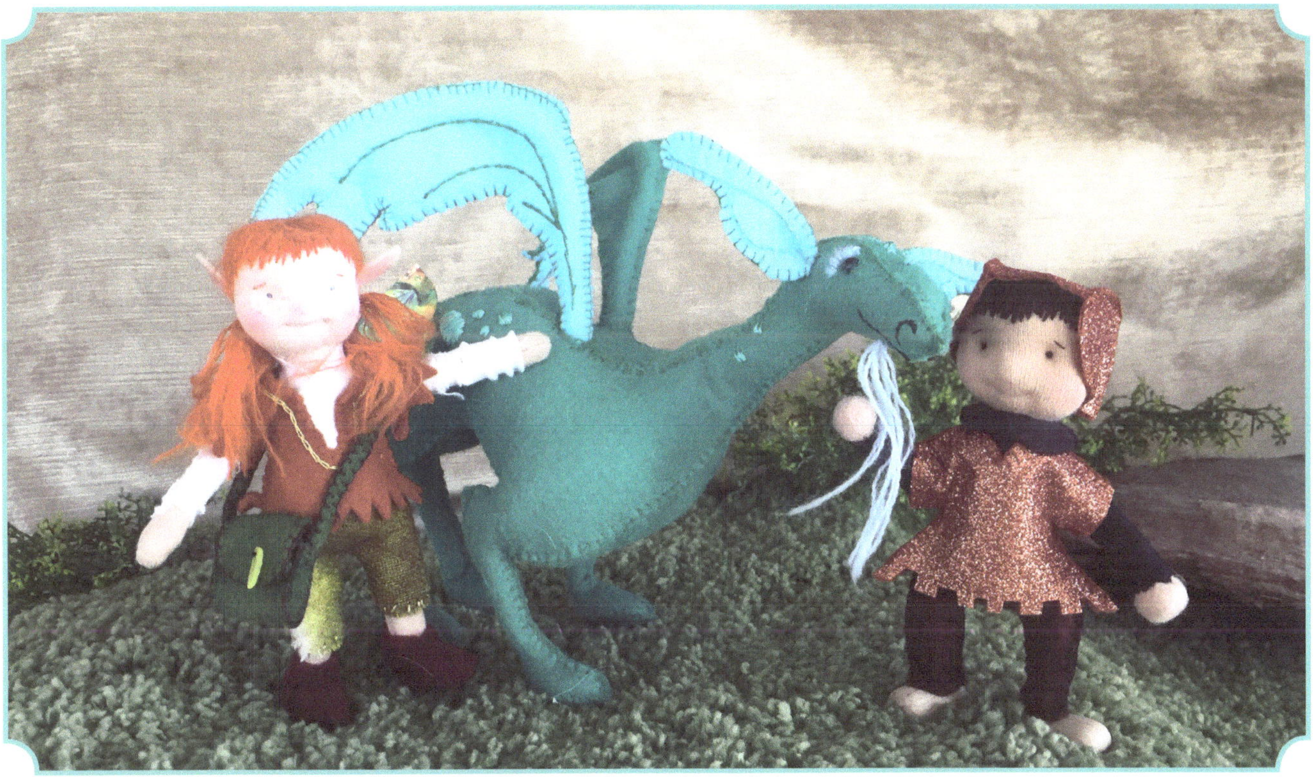

back side flap and stitch to keep in place. Repeat for other side. Stitch underarm seams.

4. Cut one collar out of black felt. Put around knight's neck and tack the front corners together.

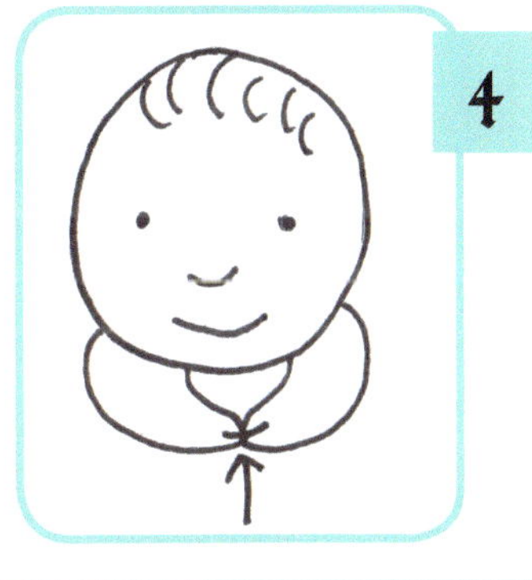

5. Cut front and back armour shirt out of metallic or glitter felt (or make your own!). With a tiny blanket stitch, sew around front neck edge. When you get to the edge, don't cut the thread, just set it aside for a moment.

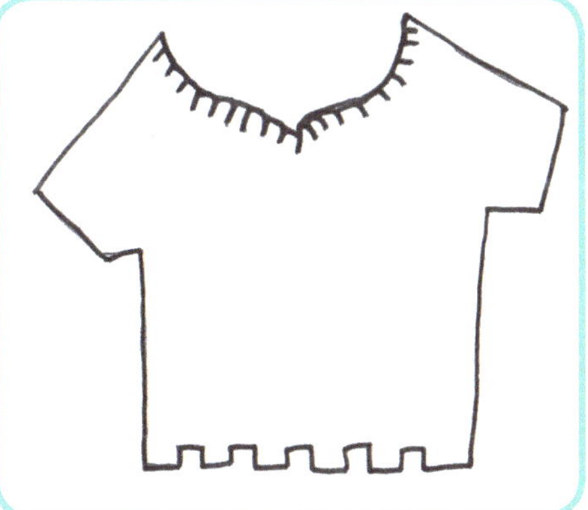

6. If you want to add a shield onto the back of your knight's armor, cut it out of felt, embroider as you wish (I embroidered a crown on the shield, but you could also do a letter or other design), and sew to middle of armor shirt back.

7. Sew the armor pieces together at one shoulder. Then slip the armour onto your knight, continue your blanket stitch around

neck edge, and sew the other shoulder while shirt is on your doll.

8. Cut two pants pieces from gray felt. Sew the inseam with a small blanket stitch.

9. Slip the pants onto your knight and stitch the outer leg seams.

10. Cut two shoe soles, two shoe uppers, and two shoe sides from felt. Stitch one shoe side to one shoe sole, matching center of shoe side to center back of sole (at notch). Repeat for other shoe.

11. Stitch shoe top to front of shoe. Repeat for other shoe. Slip shoes onto your knight.

12. Fold down the tops of the shoe sides and stitch to keep folded down. You can do any kind of decorative stitch you'd like on the shoe front to give it a little detail.

13. For your knight's helmet, you can use the metallic felt or the gray felt. I've given you a basic pattern, but it may need some adjustment because every head you create is going to be a little different! To start, cut the pattern pieces out of something soft, like a paper napkin, and test it out for fit on your knight's head. Does it look like it will fit after being sewn together? If it looks like it will be a little on the small side, make the helmet gusset piece wider and retest. Too big? Cut it down a bit.

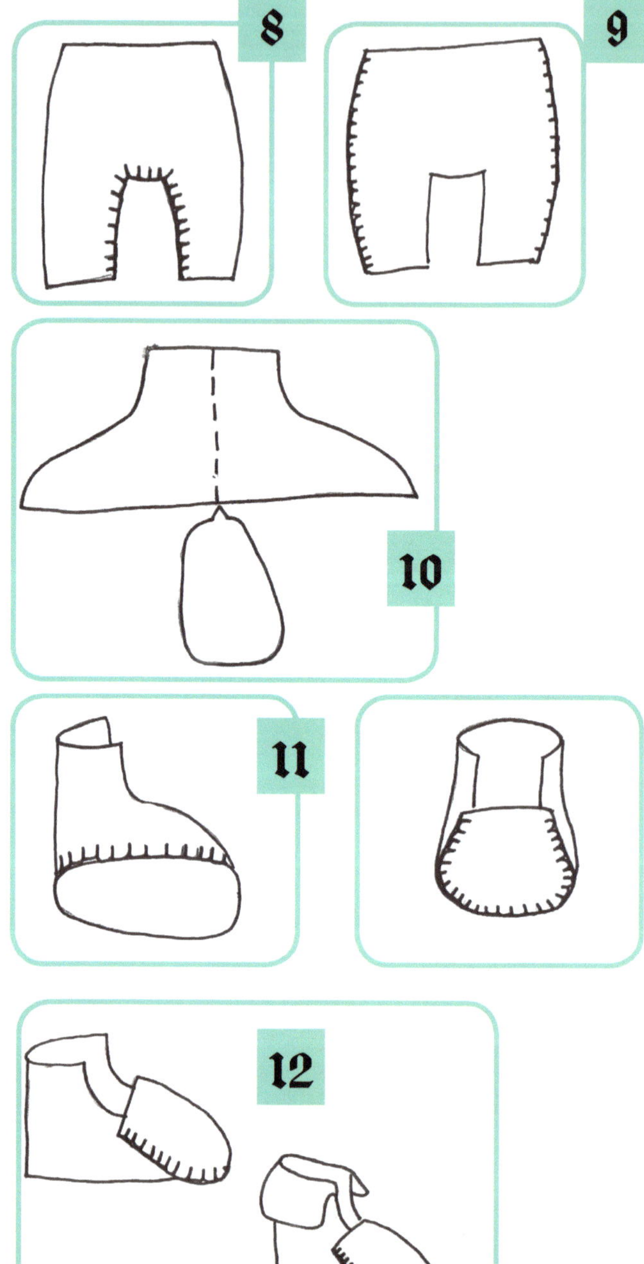

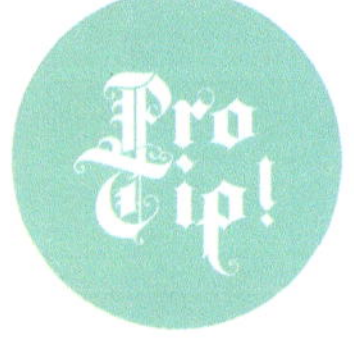

Pro-Tip: To keep your knight from losing his shoes, put a dab of tacky glue on the bottom of the wooden foot before slipping shoe on.

14. Ready to go with your pattern? Great! Cut two helmet sides and one helmet gusset out of your choice of felt.

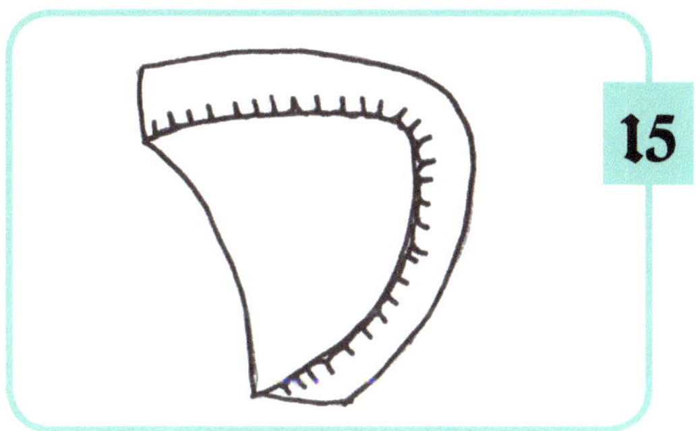

15. Stich one side of the helmet gusset to the round (notched edge) of the helmet. Knot your thread and bury end.

16. Sew the opposite side of the helmet gusset to the second helmet side. Knot and bury your thread end.

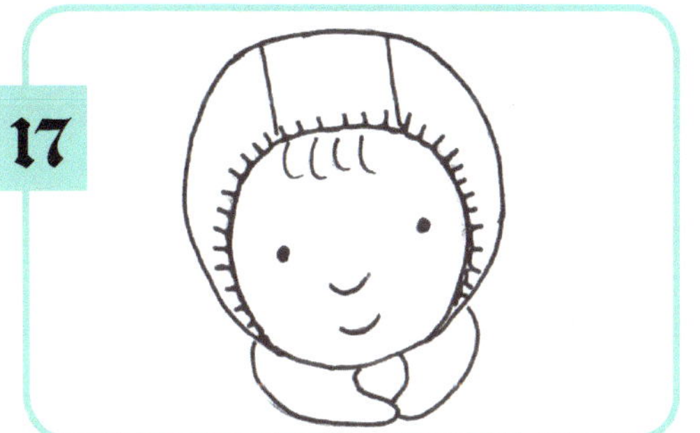

17. Place helmet on knight. With a tiny blanket stitch, sew helmet to head. Or, if you've given your knight a head full of hair, just place the helmet on your knight's head.

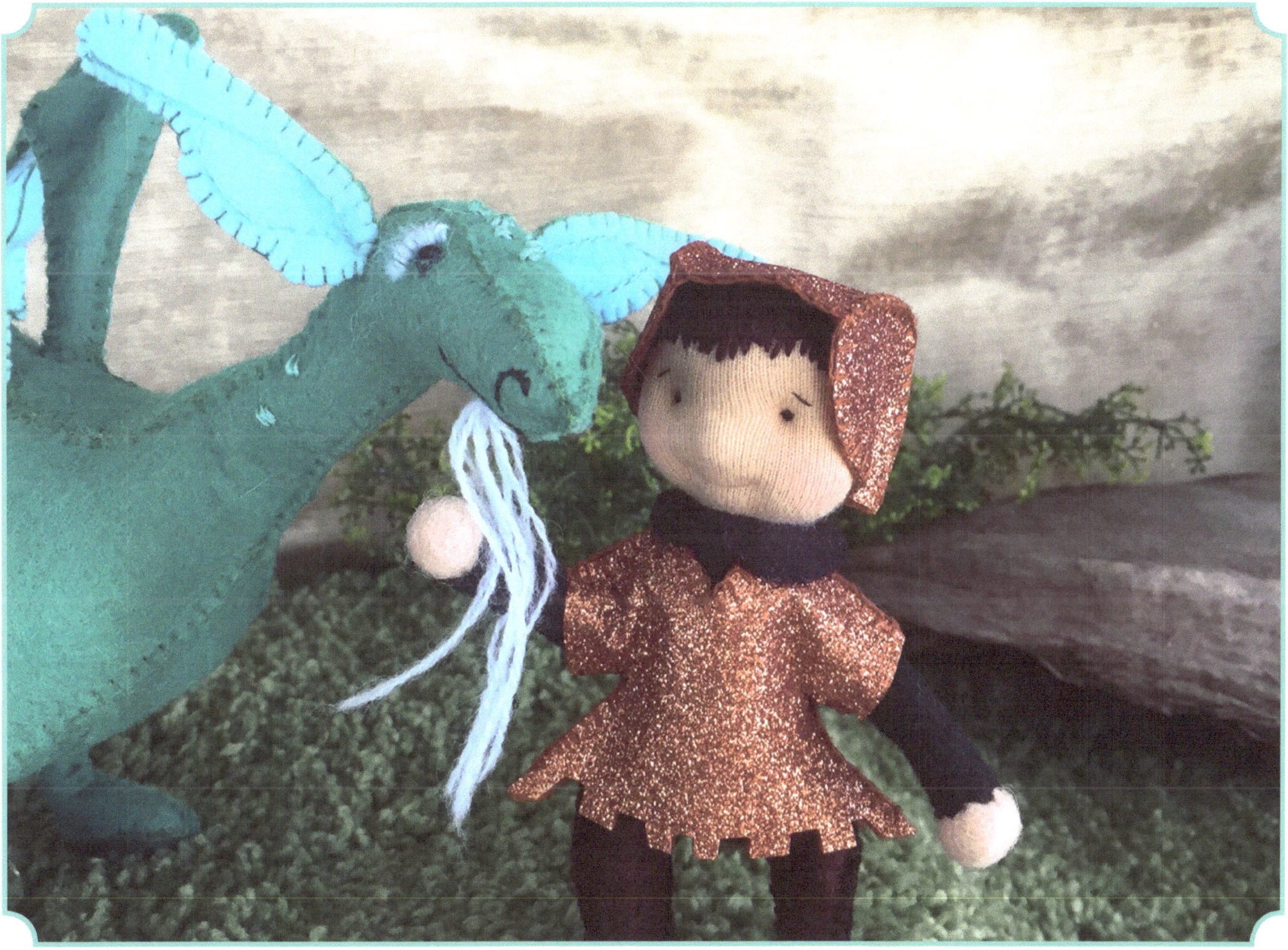

Knight's Tower

Every good knight deserves a place to rest his head!

Materials Needed:

- Two, 13"x 9" 3mm Wool felt rectangles in a stone color for tower
- Two, 8" x 12" sheet of wool felt in brown
- 8" x 12" sheet of wool felt in dark brown
- 8" x 12" sheet of wool felt in gray
- 3" x 3" Scrap of wool felt for heraldic shield
- Scrap of black wool felt for heraldic shield
- Black frog closure
- Assorted embroidery floss colors to match wool felt
- Tools
- Basic sewing supplies (see page 6)
- Plastic canvas or iron-on heavy interfacing to sturdy up tower walls and eyebrow roof

Begin by follow the directions starting on page 8 to make the freezer paper pattern pieces.

1. Cut two rectangles out of a stone color for the tower walls that measure 13" long by 9" tall. If you are using plastic canvas to make the tower walls more sturdy, cut one rectangle 1/4" smaller than your felt. If you are using iron-on interfacing, cut one rectangle 1/8" smaller than your felt pieces. If you are using interfacing bond it to one felt rectangle with a warm iron.

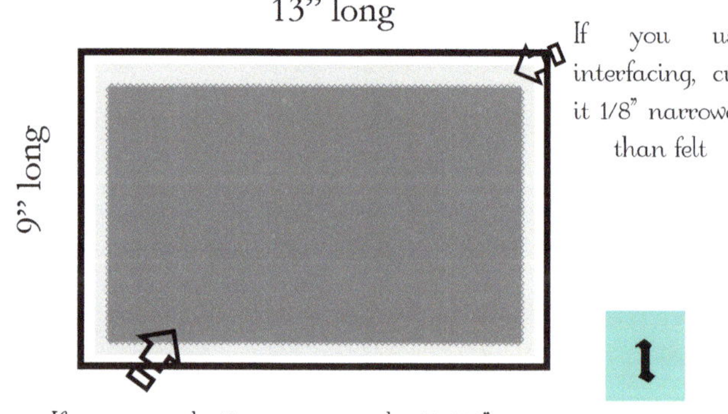

If you use plastic canvas make it 1/4" narrower than felt

2. Cut two door pieces out of brown felt. If you are using plastic canvas to make the door more sturdy, cut one door 1/4" smaller than your felt. If you are using iron-on interfacing, cut one door 1/8" smaller than your felt pieces. If you are using interfacing bond it to one felt door with a warm iron.

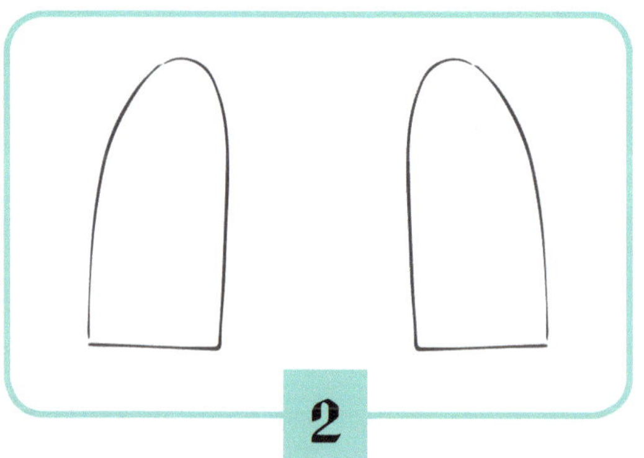

3. In the center of your tower wall, trace the door opening.
4. Cut this out of your tower wall. Line up your two rectangles, mark the door placement onto the second rectangle, and cut the second door opening.

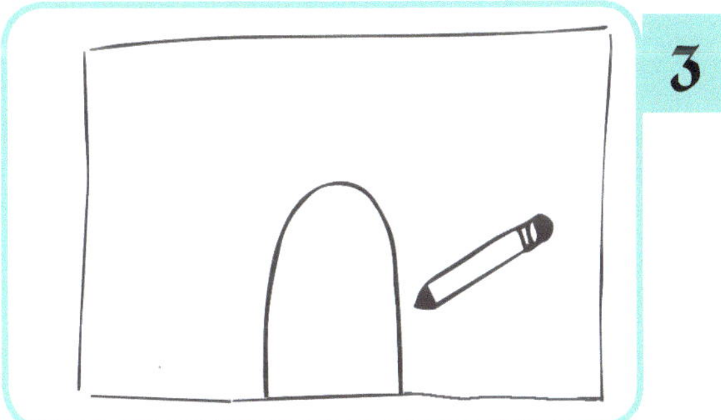

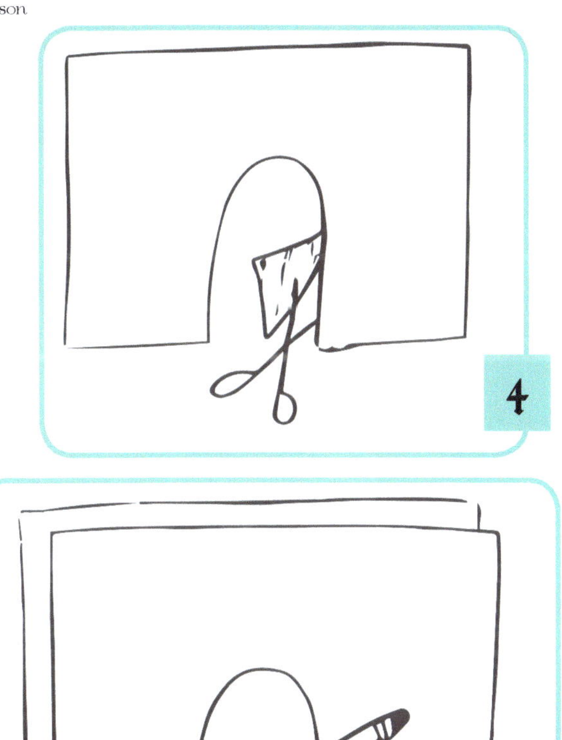

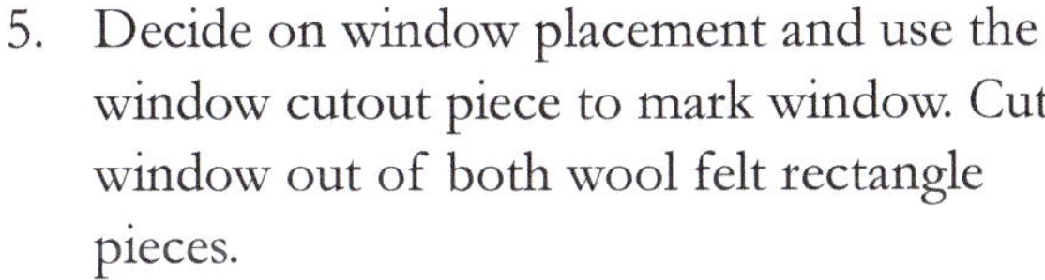

5. Decide on window placement and use the window cutout piece to mark window. Cut window out of both wool felt rectangle pieces.

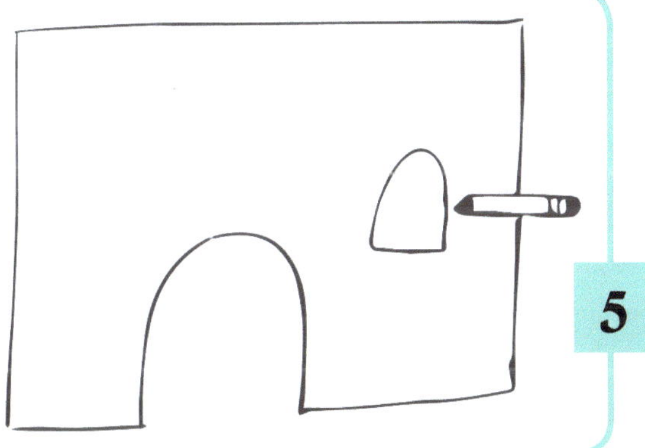

6. If you are using plastic canvas, you will need to mark the window placement and cut the window out of your canvas as well. Don't forget to cut the opening slightly larger so that the canvas won't show.

7. If you are using plastic canvas, place it between your layers of felt for the the tower wall. Pin your two tower walls together and stitch all edges, through all layers, with a blanket stitch, including the interior of the door and window. Set aside.

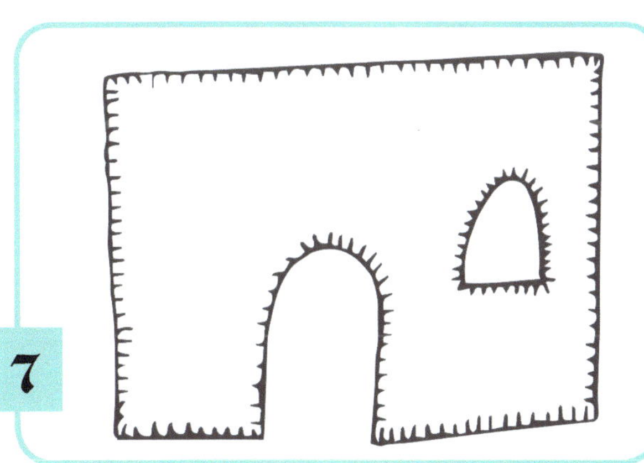

8. If you are using plastic canvas, place it between your layers of felt for the door. Pin your two doors together and stitch all edges, through all layers, with a blanket stitch.

9. Sew one edge of your door to one edge of the door opening in several places, but don't sew the whole edge. It needs some flexibility in order to open and close.

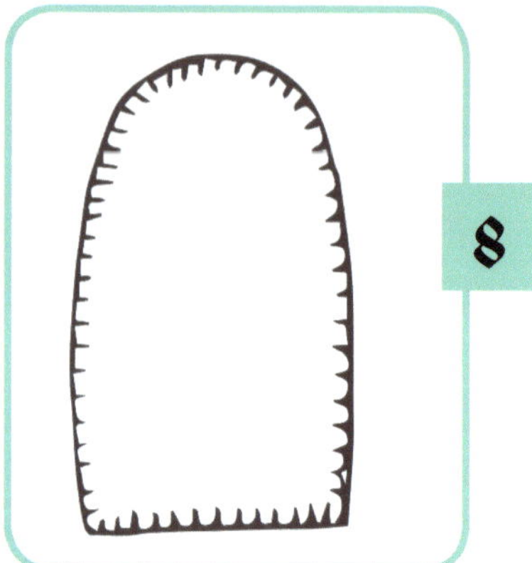

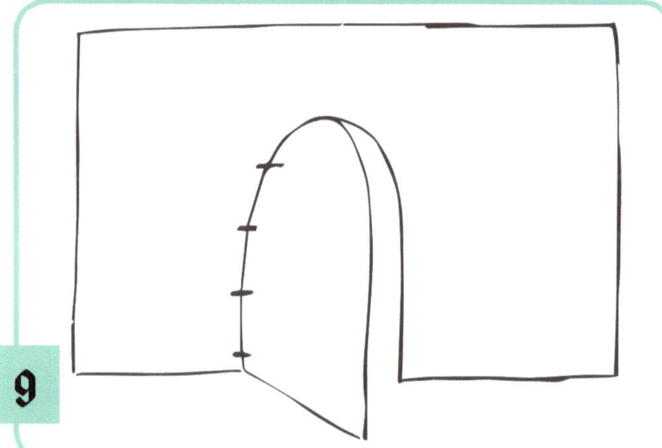

10. If you are going to add some decoration to your eyebrow roof, now is the time! Be creative—stitch your little knight's initial into it or their favorite animals, or make a shield that has stripes or dots on it. make it personal! Sew onto one eyebrow roof piece.

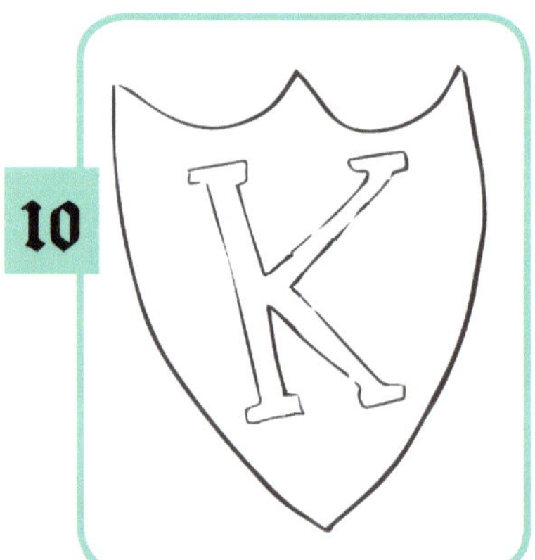

11. If you are using plastic canvas, place it between your layers of felt for the eyebrow roof. Pin your two roofs together and stitch all edges, through all layers, with a blanket stitch.

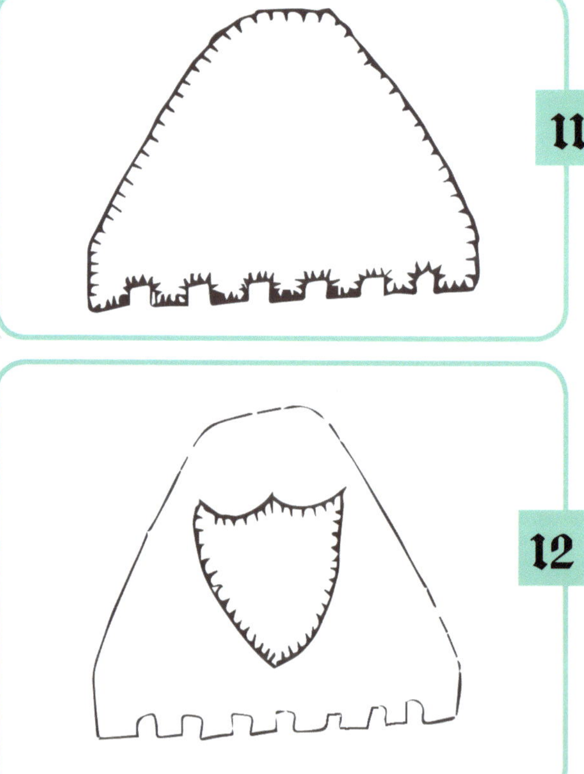

12. Stitch your decoration to the eyebrow roof. Then stitch your eyebrow roof above your door.

13. Stitch the keystone block at the top of the window. Arrange the other window bricks around window--three on the right, three at the bottom, and three on the left. Stitch in place.

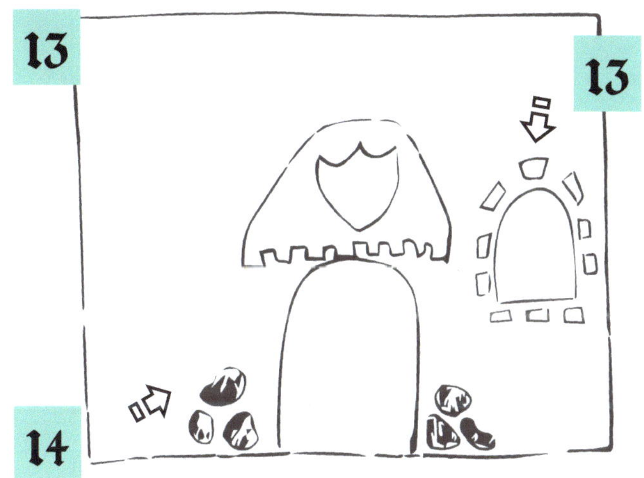

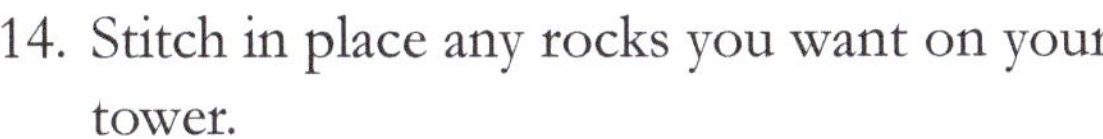

14. Stitch in place any rocks you want on your tower.

15. Stitch one flower box side to the end of each flower box piece. Repeat so that you have two.

16. Pin the two flower box pieces together and stitch the top edges together through all layers.

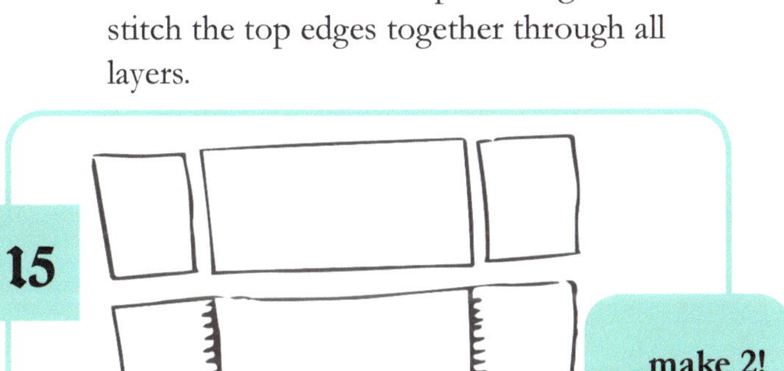

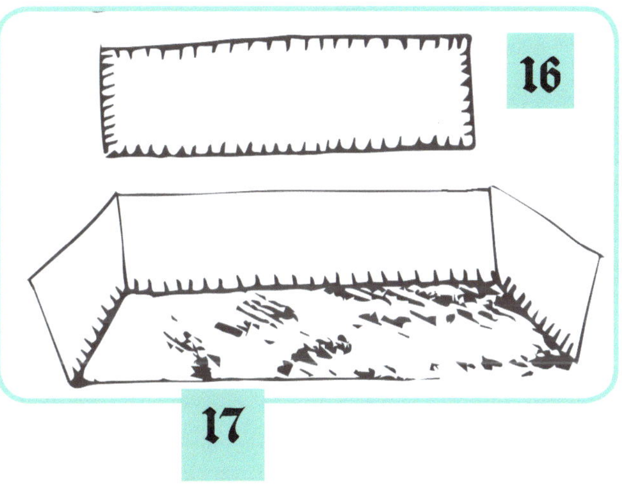

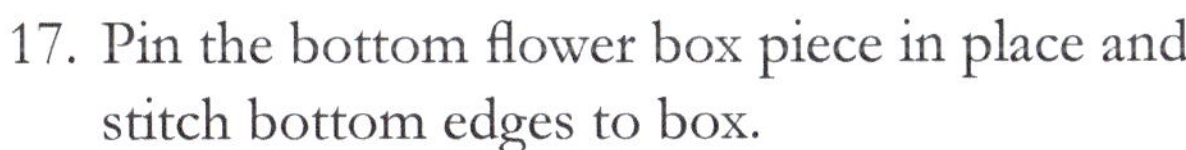

17. Pin the bottom flower box piece in place and stitch bottom edges to box.

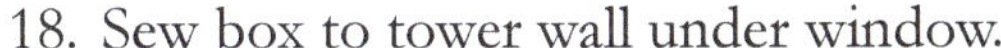

18. Sew box to tower wall under window.

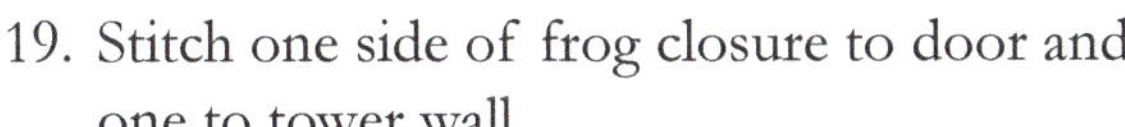

19. Stitch one side of frog closure to door and one to tower wall.

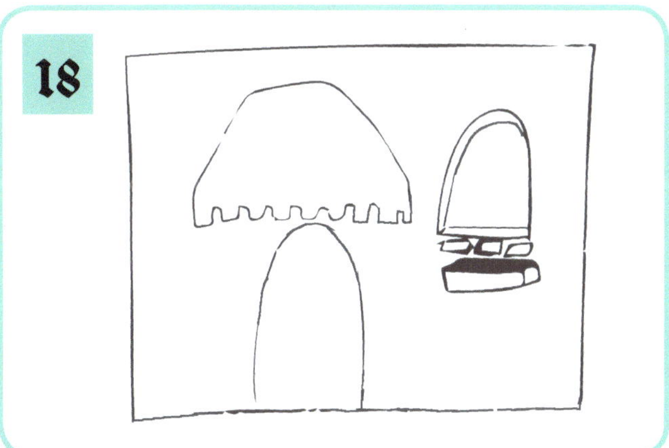

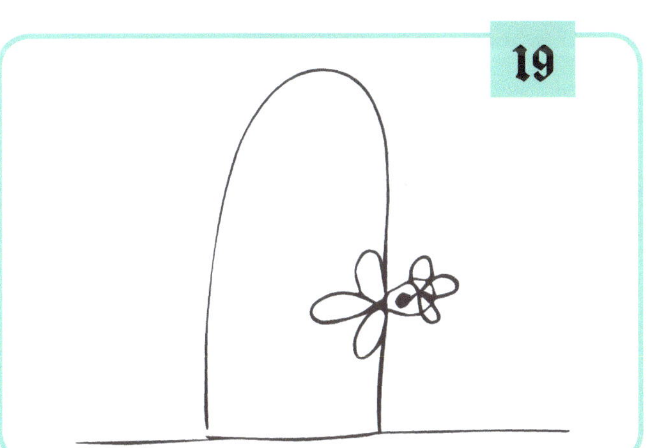

20. To finish tower roll it into a circle and sew the back edges together.

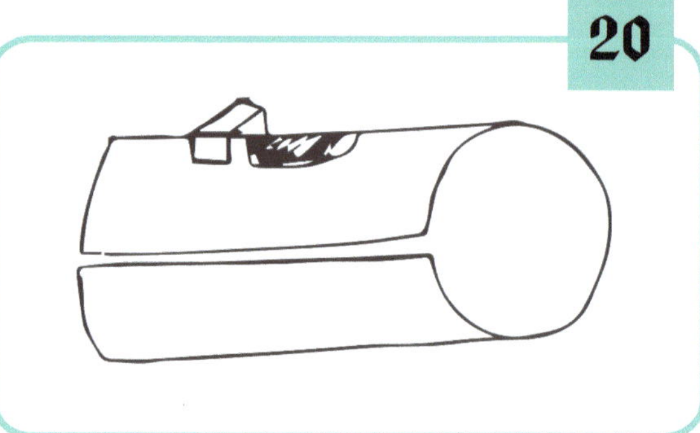

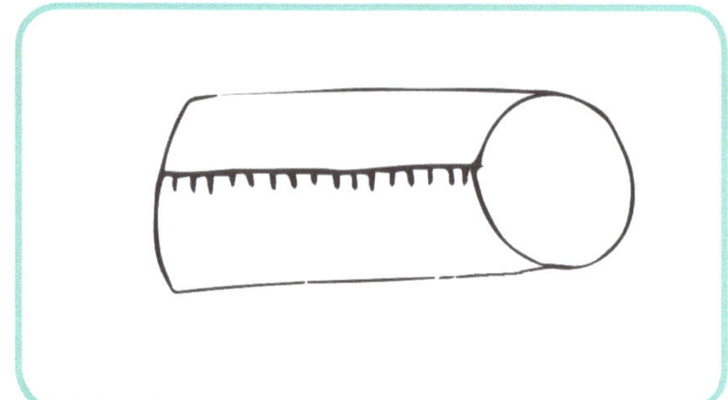

21. Cut two tower roofs, one dark brown, one the same color as your door. Cut both roofs with pinking shears on the round bottom edge.

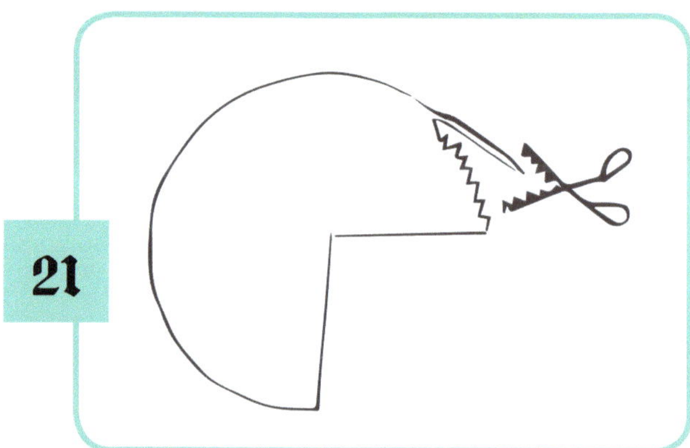

22. Layer dark brown roof on top of brown roof and stitch short sides together through all layers with a blanket stitch.

23. For added interest, sew a few shingles onto roof. You can use the window brick pattern to cut out the shingles from brown felt.

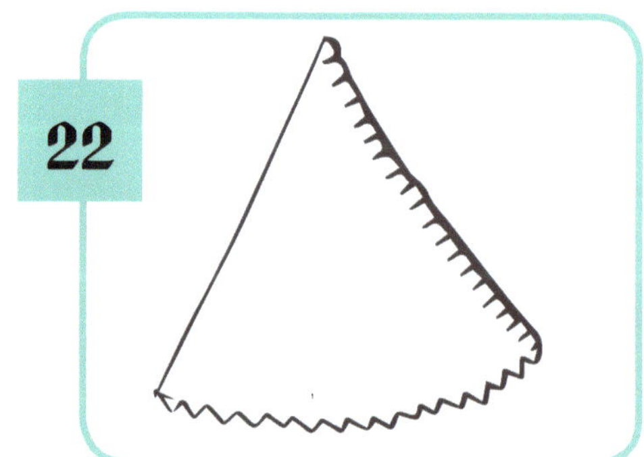

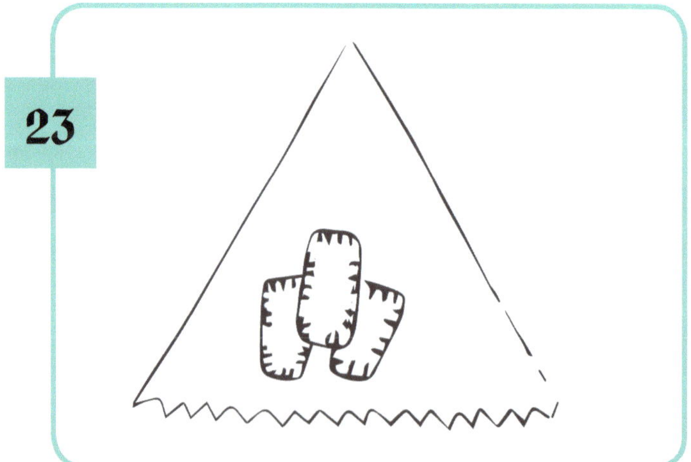

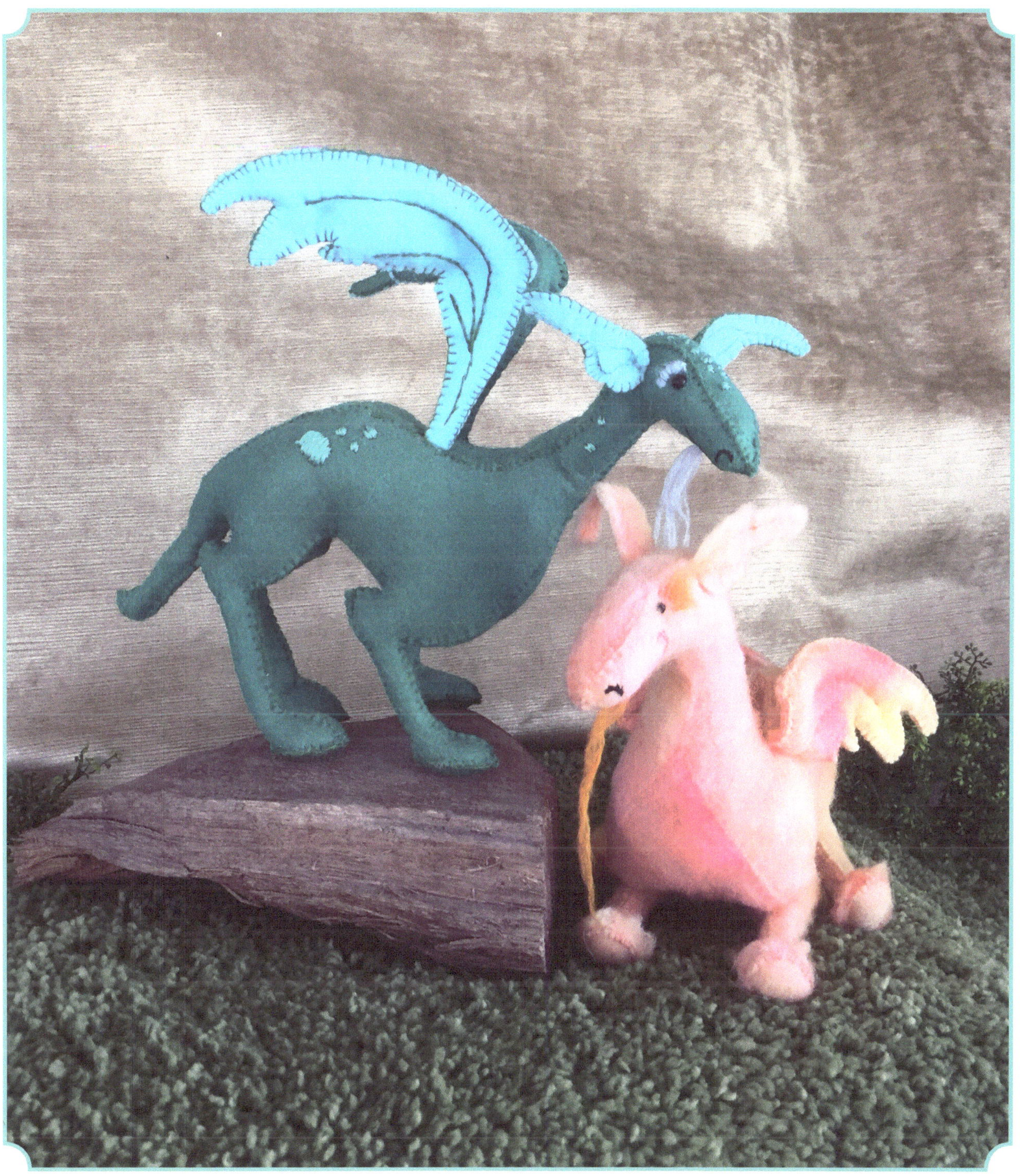

Dragons come in all sizes and colors. Have fun with your color combinations!

Faerie

A great basic body for a doll house or free play figure. So addicting to make you'll end up with a whole faerie horde!

Materials Needed:

- Cotton interlock knit in your choice of skin color
- Cotton gauze 7/8" wide x 6" long
- wool stuffing
- Binding thread
- Two 10-1/2" cotton pipe cleaners
- One 5mm wool felt ball for nose (or make your own)
- Embroidery floss for eyes
- Scraps of fabric for clothes: a mix of washed wool, wool, felt, plush cotton velour, and cottons
- Hair—any fiber will work.
- Sewing thread to match skin color and hair color
- Tools—tiny turning tubes and a small stuffing fork are highly recommended
- Heat erasable marking pen
- Basic sewing supplies (see page 6)

Optional materials for wings: cotton covered floral wire in white and Angelina fantasy film. You can also needle felt wings!

Sometimes we need a pattern that is a little more sturdy than freezer paper. Especially if you are going to use it more than a couple of times. For the faerie body, I used a manilla folder to make the pattern since it is stiff and I can trace around it easily. Trace the body pattern on a manilla folder or other stiff paper like card stock. Cut it out and set it aside while you make the head.

3

1. Cut a piece of 7/8" cotton gauze 5" long.
2. Gather one end with binding thread. Knot off and clip thread end. Turn tube right side out.
3. Wind a ball of wool roving until it measures about 5" in circumference around the middle of the ball. Keep it tight!
4. Take four, 4½" to 5" long lengths of wool roving and make a star.
5. Lay your wool ball in the center of the star.

4

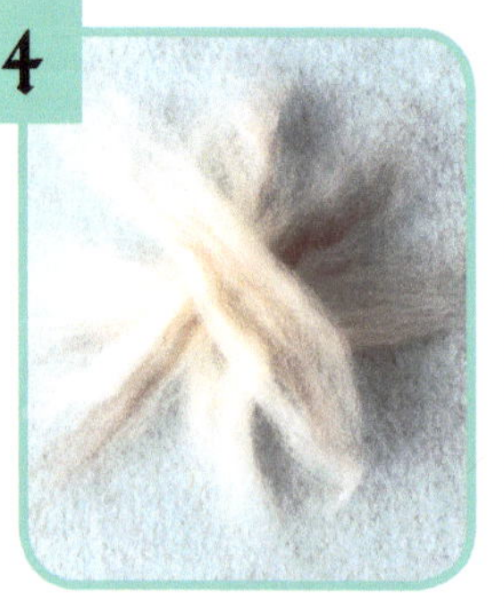

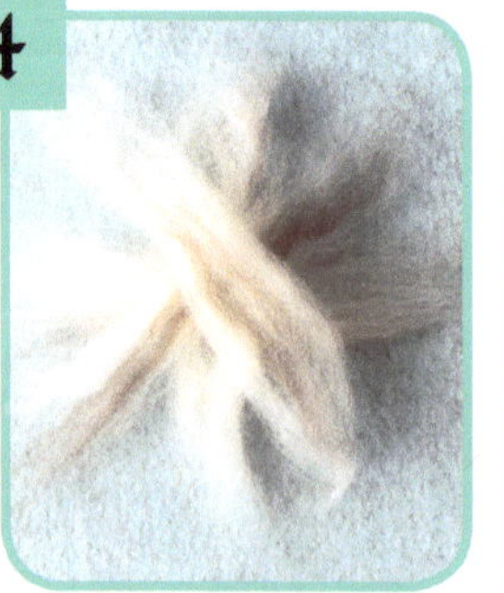

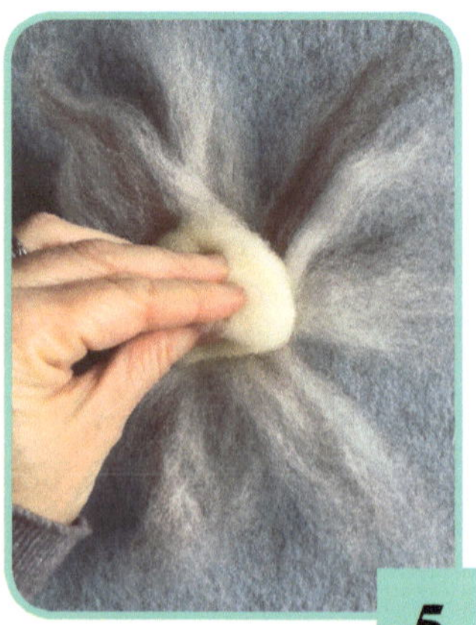

5

6. Pick it all up and pull the "legs" of the star down around the ball.

7. Insert the ball into your cotton gauze tube.

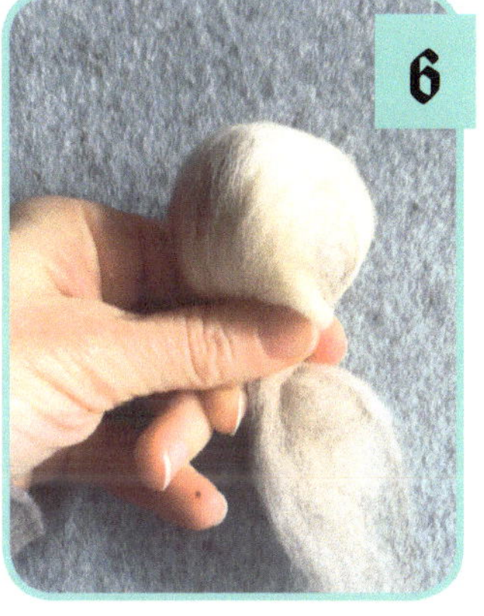

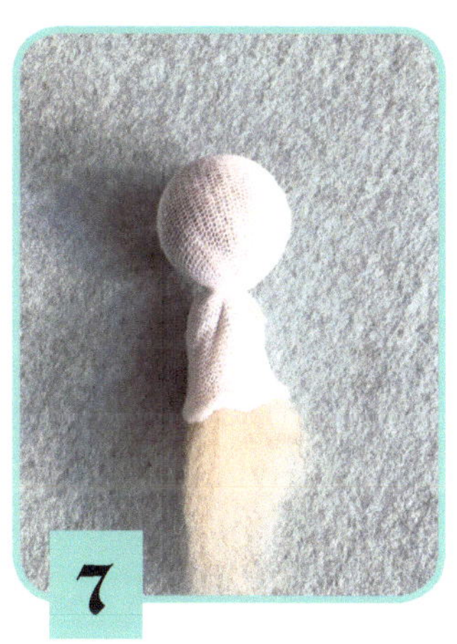

Wrap a length of binding thread just under the ball to separate the head (ball of wool) from the neck (legs of star). Tie off and snip thread end close to knot.

8. With binding thread sew neck to stiffen it up. Work in a clockwise manner, taking a stitch from 12 to 6, then 7 to 1, then 2 to 8 and so on. Sew until your dolls neck is stiff, but still a bit flexible—if you start to have trouble pushing the needle through, it's good!

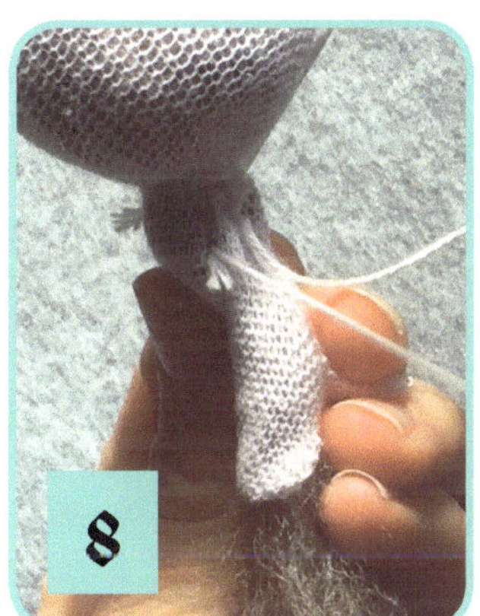

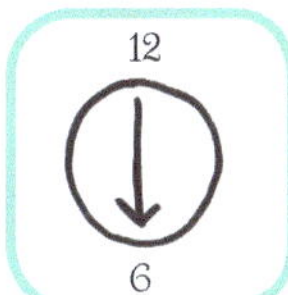

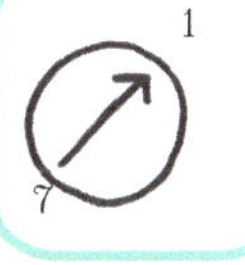

Diagram for sewing neck.

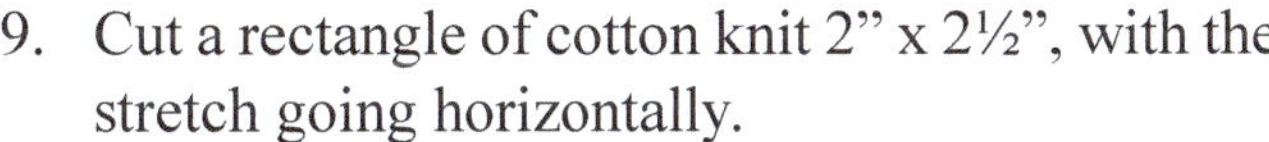

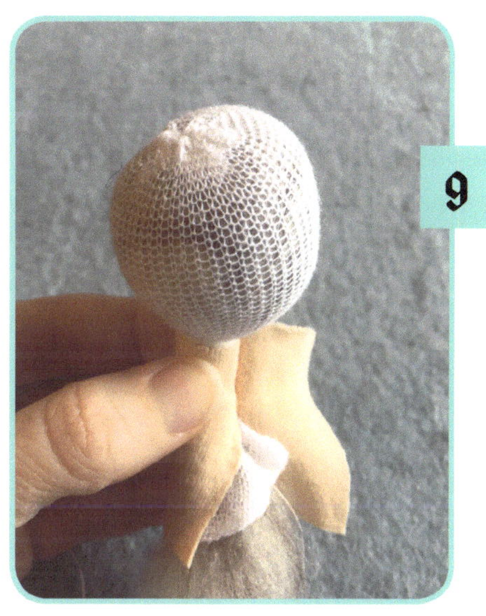

9. Cut a rectangle of cotton knit 2" x 2½", with the stretch going horizontally.

With matching thread, stitch short end to back of neck.

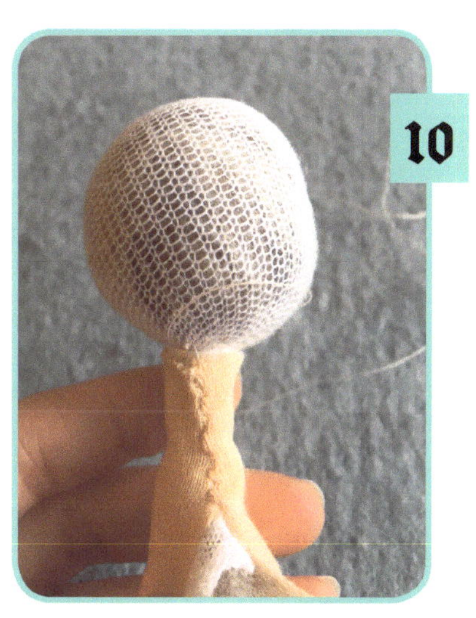

10. Stretch fabric around neck and trim any excess length off. Stitch remaining short side of fabric with a ladder stitch at back of neck.

11. Cut a rectangle 4" long x 3" wide out of cotton interlock knit (with stretch going horizontally). Sew up short side of rectangle with a ¼" seam. Turn tube RSO.

12. Slip cotton knit tube on head with seam at the back of head. Tuck under ¼" of the bottom edge.

13. With your matching thread gather the bottom edge of the tube by taking gathering stitches in the fold of fabric.

14. Gently pull stitch to gather bottom edge of head. Knot and tie off, but don't cut your thread. With a ladder stitch sew bottom edge of head skin to neck skin. Knot thread and bury end.

15. Make a crease with your fingernail at the line you want to place your eyes (about the middle of the face). Insert a small (5mm) wool ball or pompom between the skin layer and the cotton gauze head just below this line.

16. Pull top of head skin up so that it is tight. Pin so that it stays in place.

Trim excess skin fabric off close to pin.

17. Beginning in center of head, stitch head skin together using a ladder stitch. When you reach the end, stitch back toward the center and continue to the opposite end.

18. You will have two little points at each end. Stitch those down flat, but don't worry about it too much as you will cover them with hair.

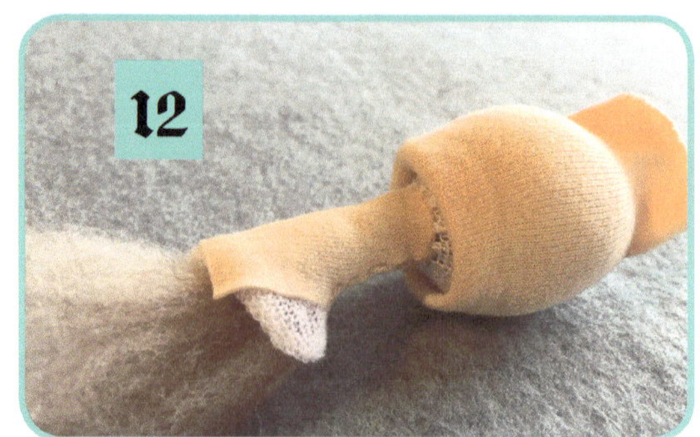
12

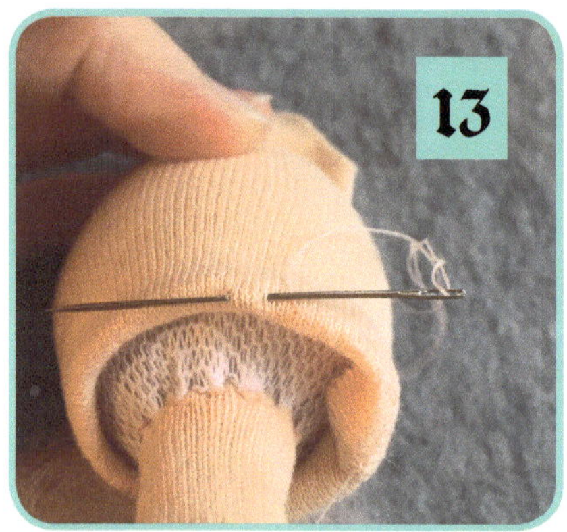
13

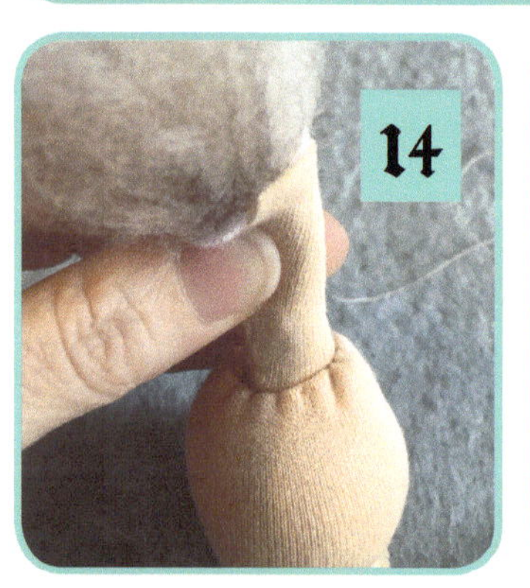
14

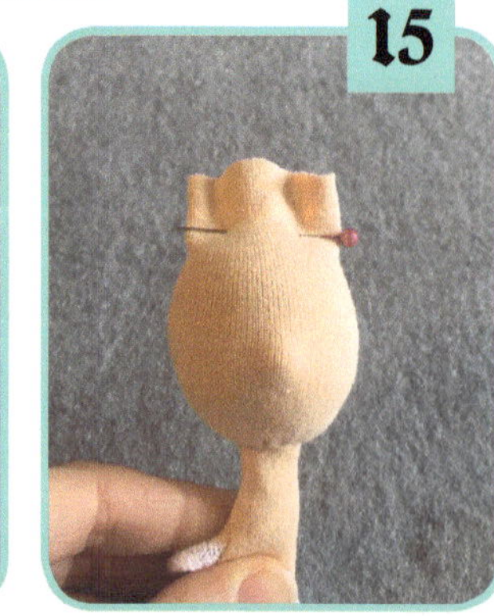
15

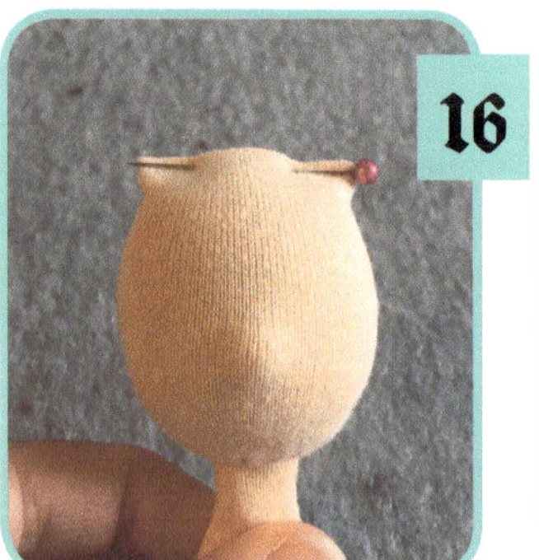
16

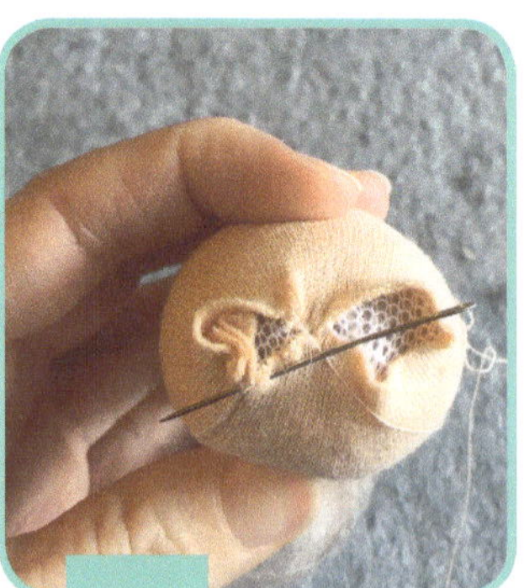
17

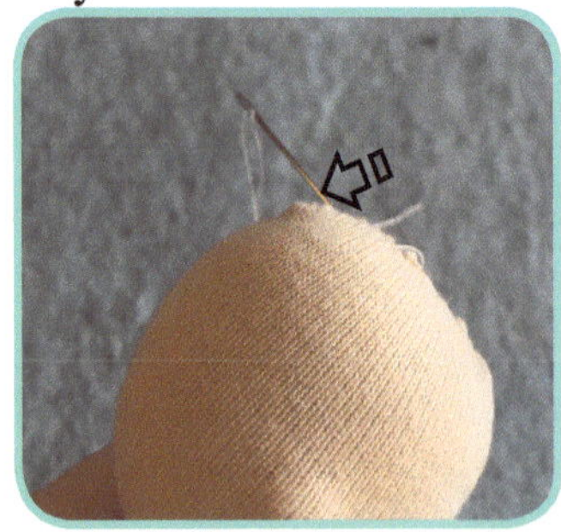

19. Use two pins to mark eye placement.
Knot matching thread on top of head and insert needle into head and out at the first pin. Remove pin. Move needle over a couple of threads and reinsert needle into fabric, and out through the top of the head. Pull thread gently.

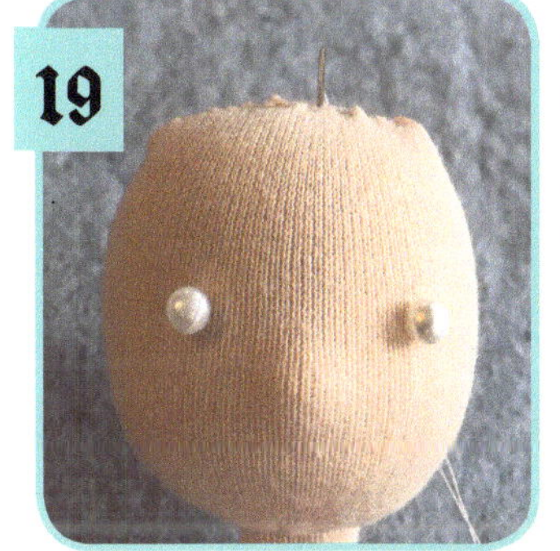

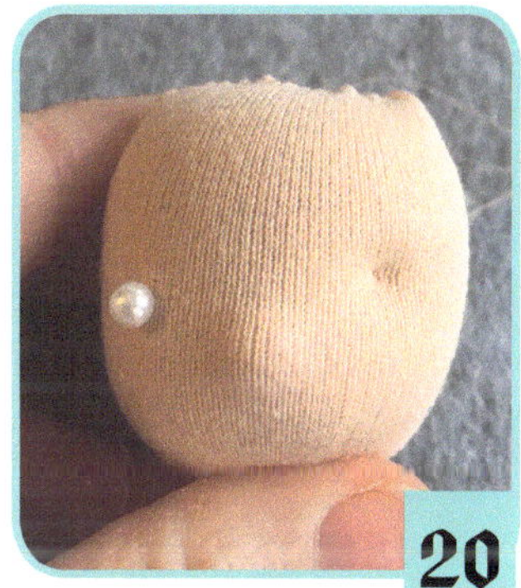

Repeat for second eye. Repeat again for both eyes to further sculpt and define.

20. To further sculpt face, insert needle back into top of head and exit at eye. Reinsert at eye and exit directly under eye at the edge of the neck (under the "chin").

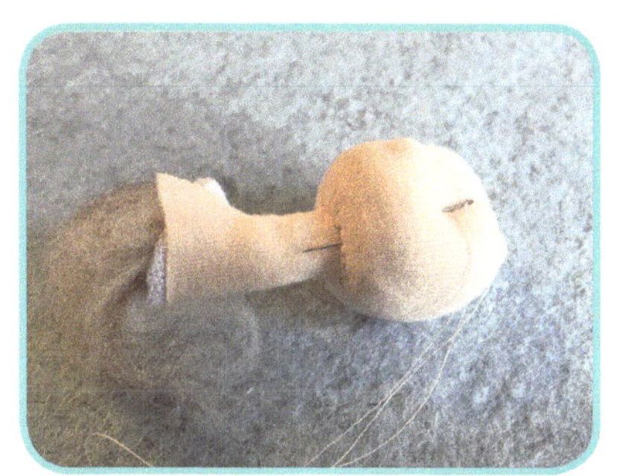

21. Move the needle over a few threads, reinsert into fabric and exit at eye. Repeat until satisfied with sculpting. Then repeat the process for the other side of the face. When satisfied with both sides of the face, knot thread in the top of the head, but don't cut.

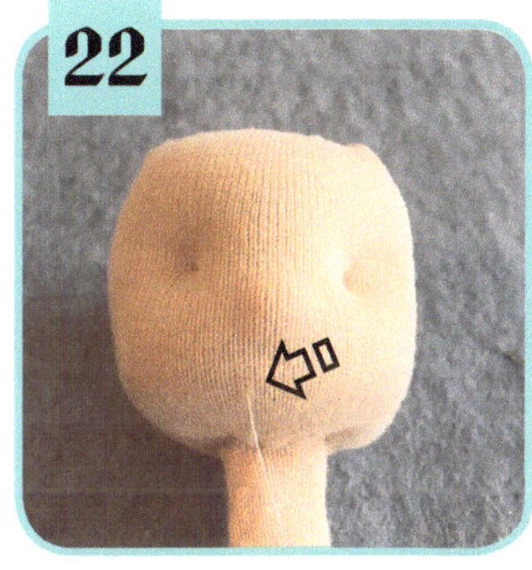

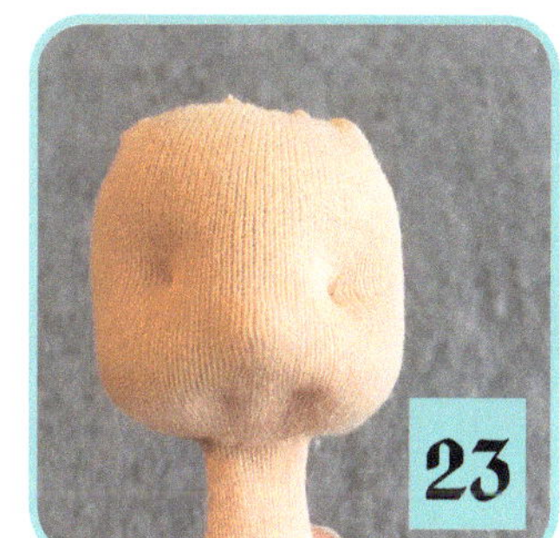

22. To make your doll's expression insert the needle through the top of the head and exit ½ way between nose and chin at the outer edge of the nose.

23. Reinsert the needle and exit at the opposite eye. Repeat steps above for second mouth corner. When finished sculpting, exit needle at top of head and knot, burying thread end.

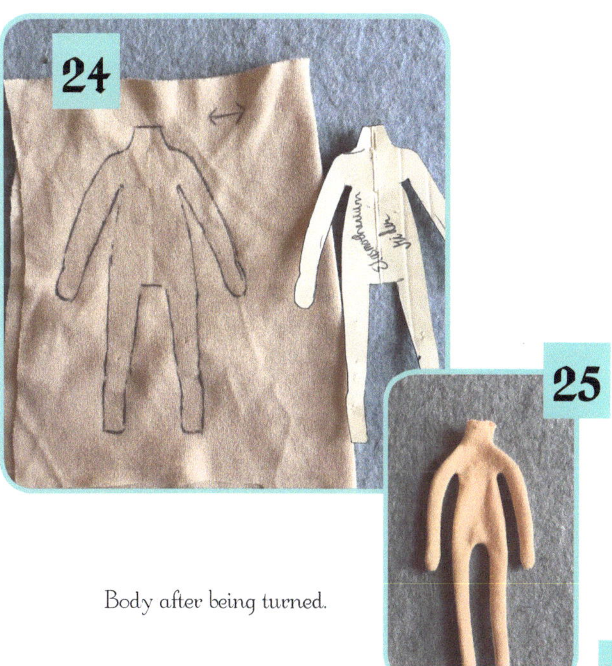

Body after being turned.

24. For the body, trace the body with a heat erasable marking pen onto a double layer of cotton knit with the stretch going horizontal across the body.

25. Sew on the line. For best results use a jersey needle in your sewing machine.

Cut the body out about 1/8" from the sewing line. Using a hair dryer or warm iron, erase the pen markings. Turn body RSO. A set of tiny brass turning tubes are indispensable for turning tiny parts. See the sources section for suppliers.

26. To give your doll a posable skeleton, use 10½" long chenille stems.

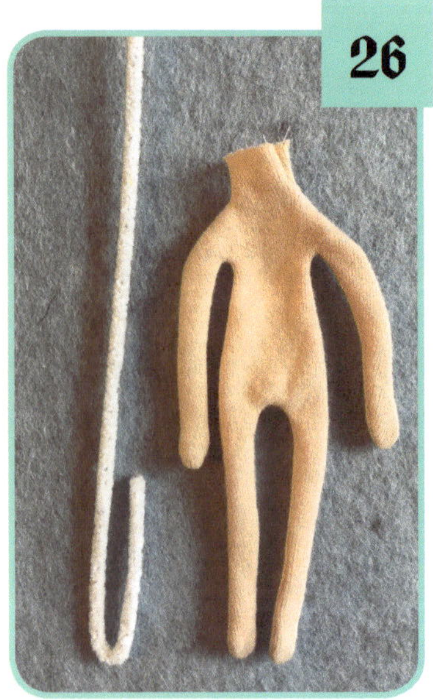

27. Bend one end of a chenille stem up about 2". Twist the stem together.

28. Wrap a bit of wool roving around the sharp end of the chenille stem. Push the wrapped end into one leg, letting the remaining length of the chenille stem hang out of the neck. Repeat process for second leg.

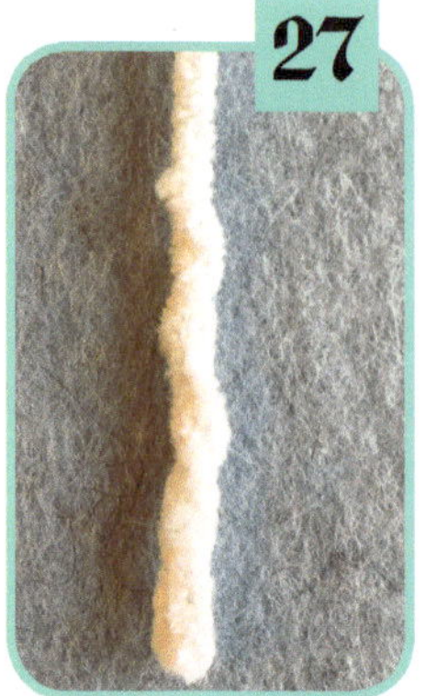

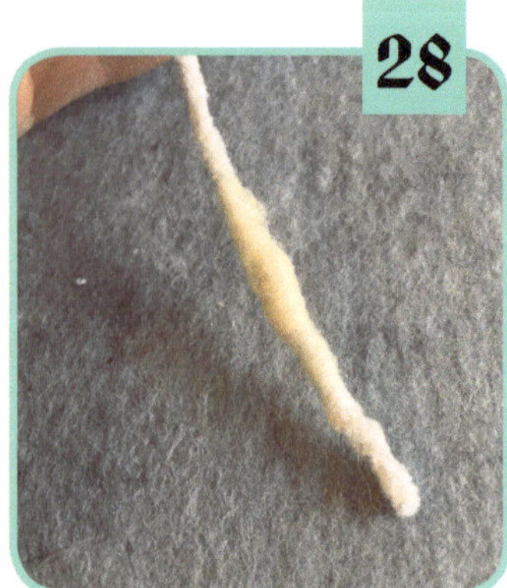

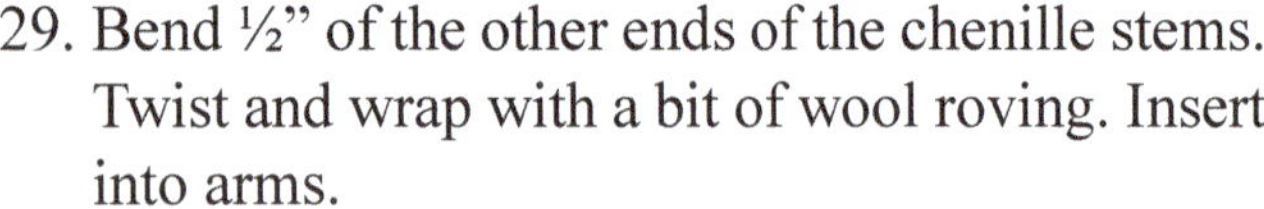

29. Bend ½" of the other ends of the chenille stems. Twist and wrap with a bit of wool roving. Insert into arms.

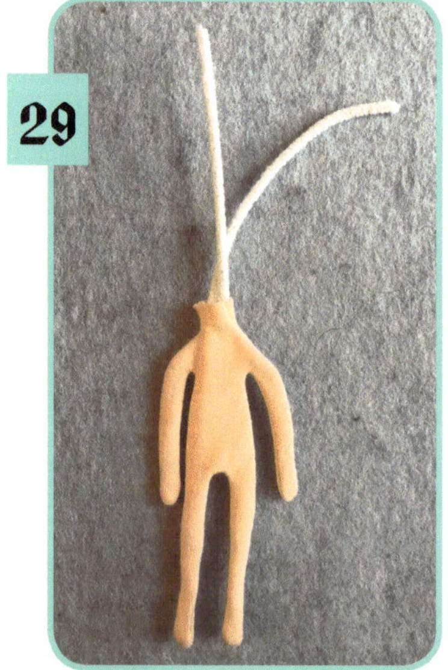

30. Stuff the top of the foot of each leg. Don't overstuff, and don't stuff what will be the bottom of the foot. For easy placement of your stuffing, use a tiny stuffing fork and small bits of wool stuffing at a time.

31. After stuffing the foot, bend the foot portion of the leg at a 90-degree angle.

Continue to stuff both the back and the front of the leg and body up to the "arm pits".

Now stuff the arms, again using small bits of wool as you work.

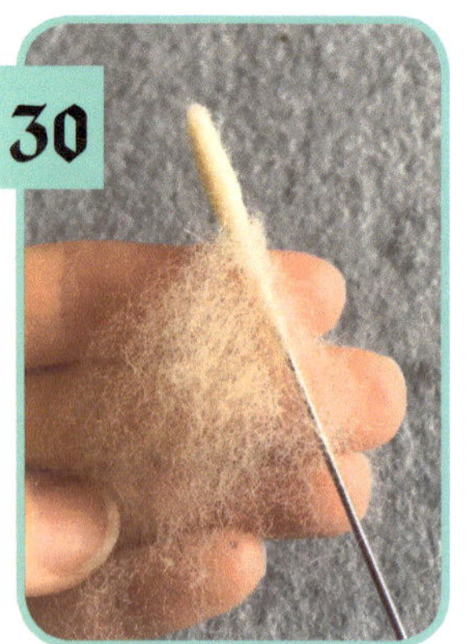

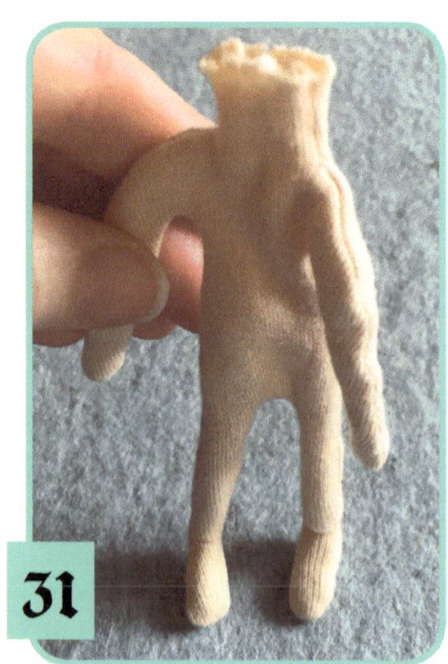

32. Now pick up the beautiful head and neck you made earlier. Pull out any excess wool roving from the neck and trim off any excess length of cotton knit fabric.

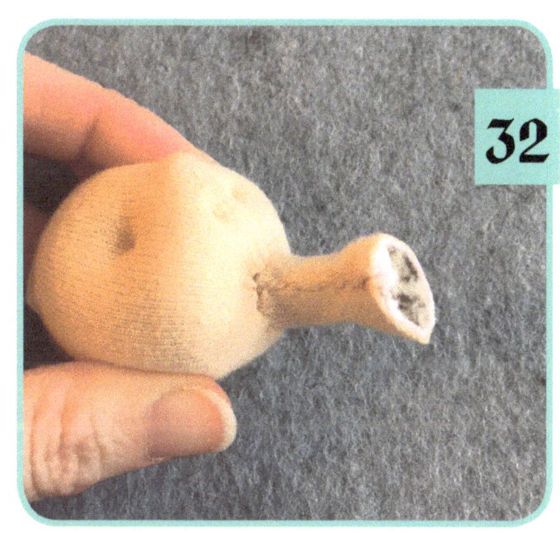

33. This next part is a bit tricky! You need to push the neck of the head into the neck of the body. You may need to use your stuffing fork to help pull the neck skin over the neck.

Finish stuffing any little holes that were left in the chest and back area.

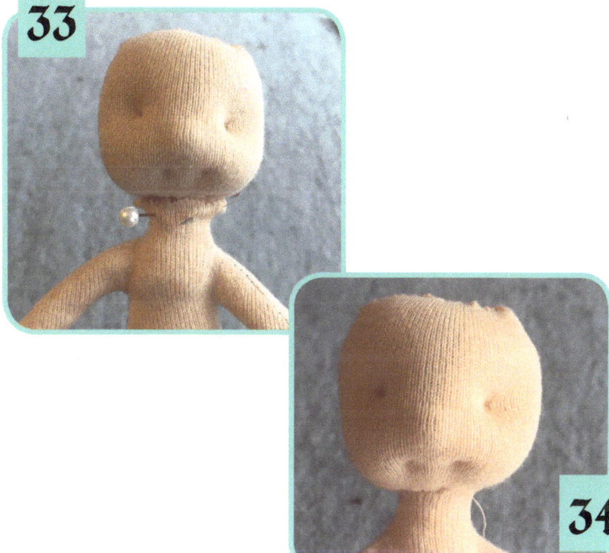

34. Ladder stitch the head to the neck skin under the chin at neckline. Knot and bury thread at back of neck.

35. For a final touch on the feet, knot thread in middle of folding line on foot. Exit needle at side seam.

Ladder stitch by inserting the needle just above and then just below the folding line and then pull the stitches together gently. Essentially, you will be pulling the skin together over the folding line.

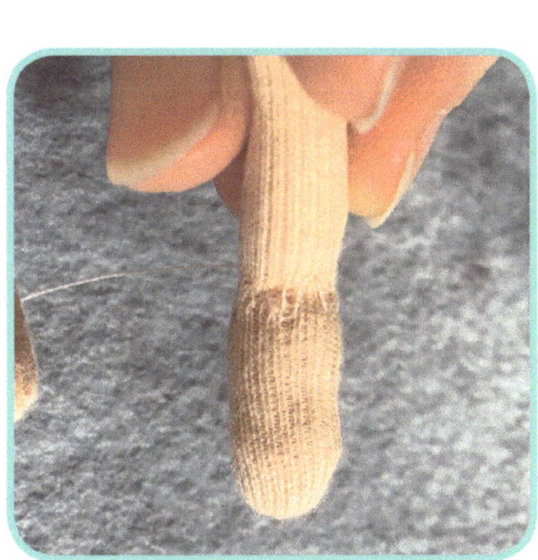

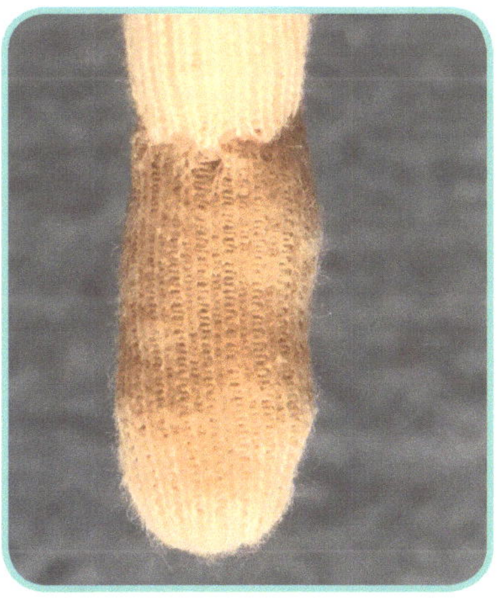

36. When you get to the other side seam, pull stitches tight and knot thread. Bury end. Repeat for other foot.

Pro Tip!

Pro-Tip: As hard as you might try to make your face perfectly symmetrical, it doesn't always happen. Embrace it! These small asymmetries give your character personality.

37. To embroider the eyes knot 5 strands of embroidery floss in the color of your choice in the back of the head. Insert needle and exit at eye. Make a French knot with needle exiting at the back of the head. Repeat for second eye. Knot floss and bury end. Add eyebrows with one strand of floss in a similar color as hair.

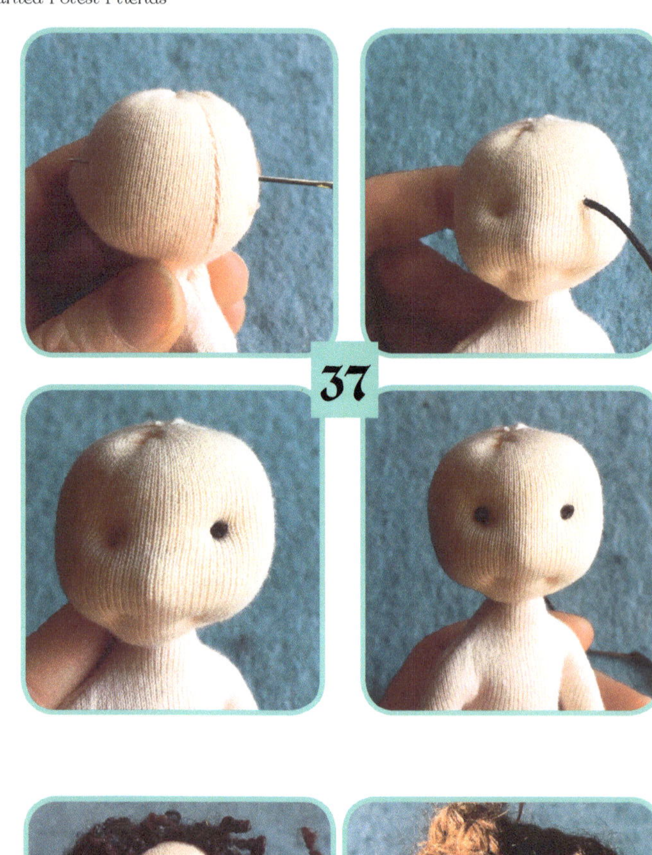

38. For the fairy pictured below, I used the Genziana wool thread and embroidered her hairstyle, then sewed on loops of thread for her pigtails. To give it a bit of a mussed look, I brushed the thread with a bunka brush.

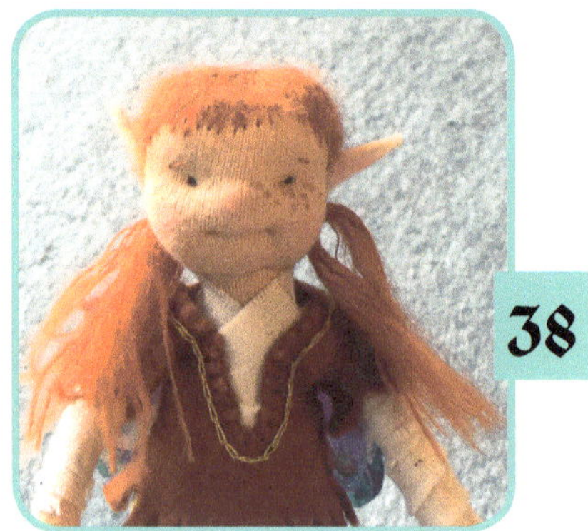

Doll hair is a great way to get creative. You can embroider hair on to your doll's head with wool thread, embroidery floss, or other yarn.

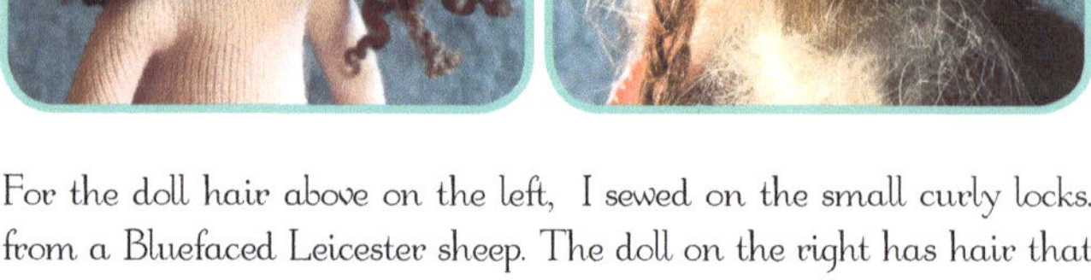

For the doll hair above on the left, I sewed on the small curly locks from a Bluefaced Leicester sheep. The doll on the right has hair that is wool thread that I braided and then sewed onto the head.

You can also sew on wool locks or make a wig out of Tibetan lamb hair. There are so many ways to get creative when it comes to giving your doll hair! If you know how to knit or crochet, there are many tutorials online that will teach you how to make a wig cap for a traditional Waldorf style wig.

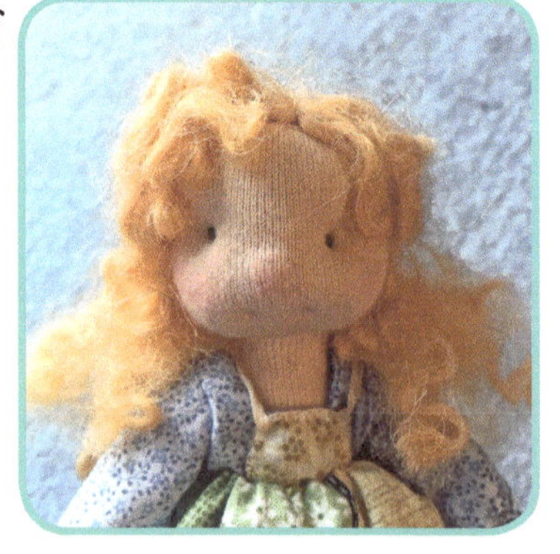

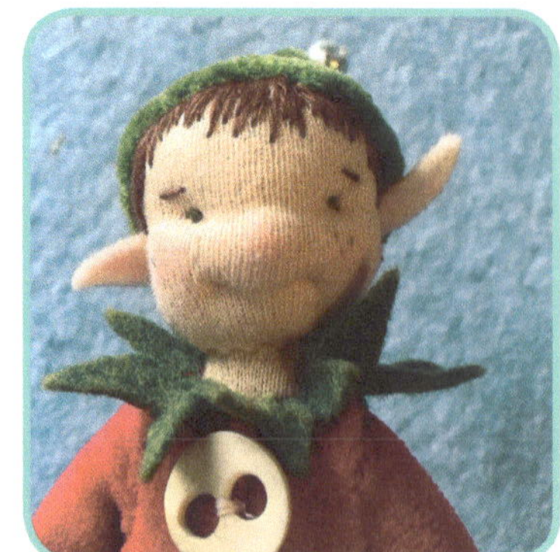

The hair for the doll on the left is braided wool that is sewn on. The doll on the right is Genziana wool thread embroidered onto the head without being brushed.

Faerie ears, blush, and freckles

1. To give your faerie pointy ears, cut two ears from wool felt that matches your skin tone and sew onto the head with matching thread.

2. To give your faerie blushed cheeks you can use a colored pencil in a pinky-blush color. A Prismacolor marker is a great tool to add freckles.

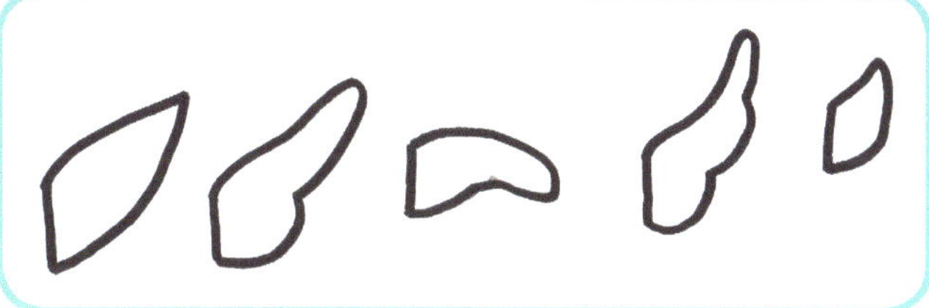

Try these ear shapes or draw your own!

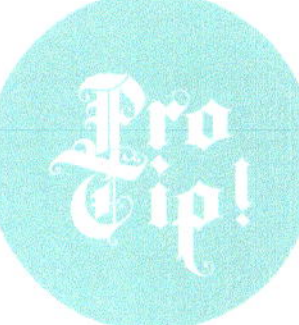

Pro-tip: The bottom of the ears should be placed in line with the bottom of the nose.

Faerie Wings

1. To make the optional wings for your faerie, trace with a Sharpie marker the outside line of the wing onto one piece of the Angelina fantasy film long enough to cover the wing pattern.

2. Cut two pieces of white cotton-covered floral wire the same length as the veins drawn on the wing pattern.

3. Put a bit of glue on your wire and set in place carefully on your film. Repeat for second vein.

4. Place the second length of film on top of first length, sandwiching the floral wire in between the two sheets.

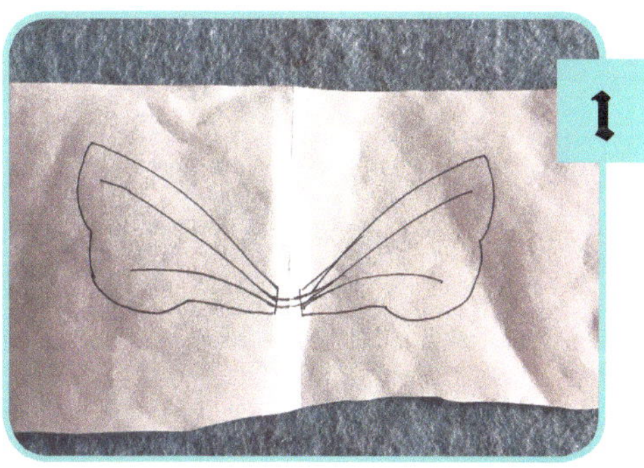

1

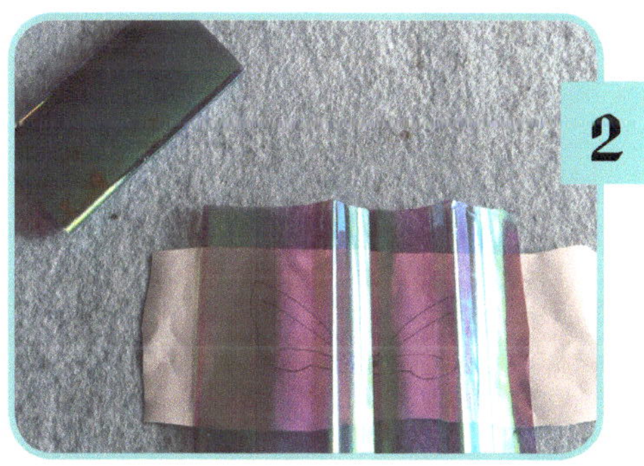

2

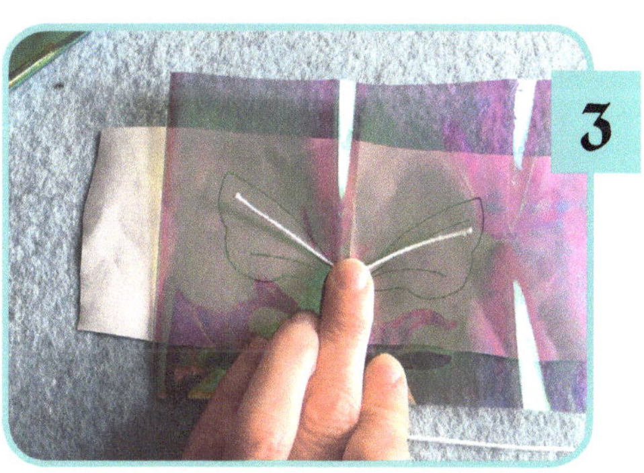

3

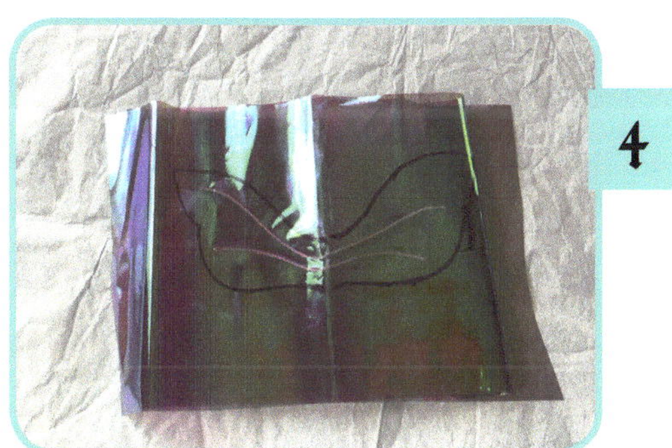

4

5. Place a heavy book on top of your wings and let dry for a couple of hours.

6. When dry, place wings under a pressing sheet, or white dishtowel, and press with a warm iron. The fantasy film will stick to itself and the colors will pop and become more iridescent.

7. Cut your wings out just inside the drawn Sharpie line. Set aside until your faerie is dressed.

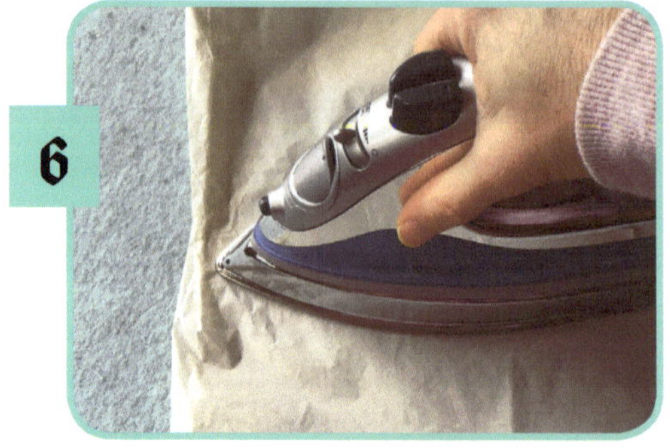

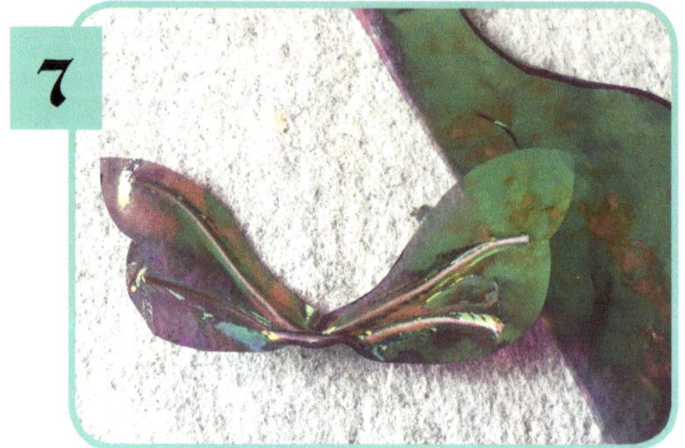

Dress your faerie

To make tights:

Cut two tights patterns out of an old sock or other cotton knit. Using a 1/8" seam allowance and matching thread, stitch pieces together beginning at the waist, continuing down the leg, around the toe, through the inseam, down the second leg, around the toe and back up the second leg to the waist. Make a narrow hem at the waist. Turn RSO and slip onto your faerie. If the waist is a little baggy, gather with your thread and pull to fit. Knot thread and bury end.

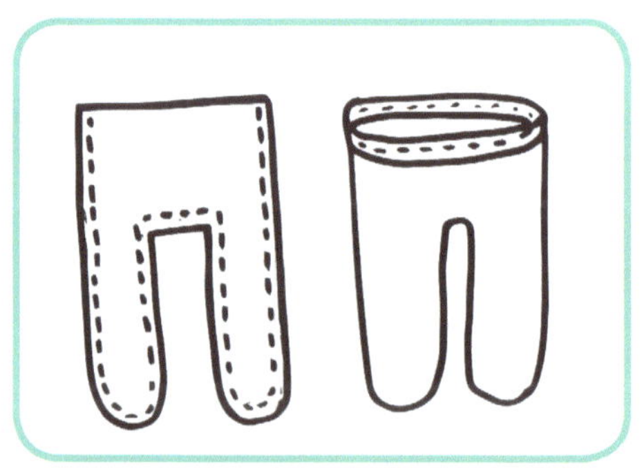

To make the jumper:

Cut one faerie jumper out of plush cotton velour. Cut the back side down the middle about 1-1/2", following the dotted line on the pattern.

Cut two sleeves out of cotton plush velour.

1. Sew the right side of one sleeve to one jumper at armhole with a 1/8" seam allowance. Repeat for second sleeve.

2. Fold the jumper in half with right sides together and pin. Stitch with a 1/8" seam allowance starting at the wrist, through the armpit, and down the outside of the leg. Repeat for opposite side of jumper.

3. Pin and stitch the inseam of the jumper again with a 1/8" seam allowance.

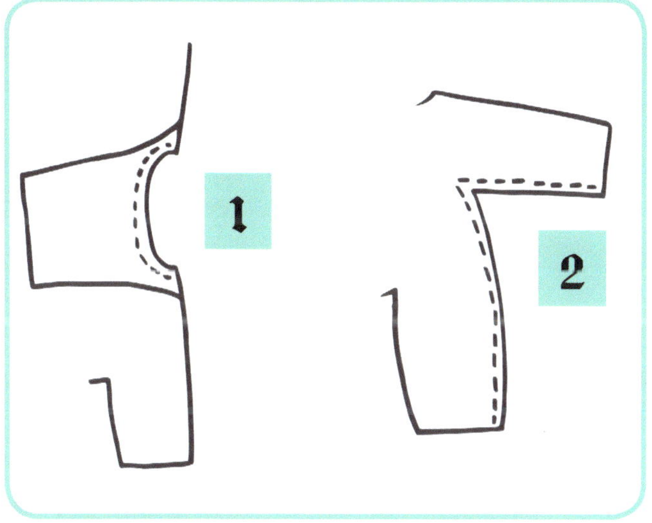

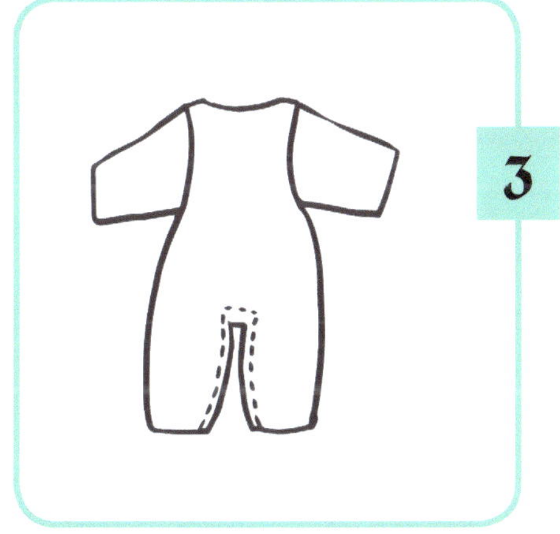

Pro Tip! Cotton Velour is very soft and slippery. Pin it well! Alternatively, you could use a recycled wool sweater for the jumper.

Turn jumper right side out and slip onto your doll.

Sew up the back slit with matching thread and a ladder stitch.

Roll under a narrow hem at the legs and wrists. With a tiny ladder stitch, sew the hems.

Stitch the collar on at the neck.

Add any embellishments to the jumper that you wish to add, keeping in mind the age of the child.

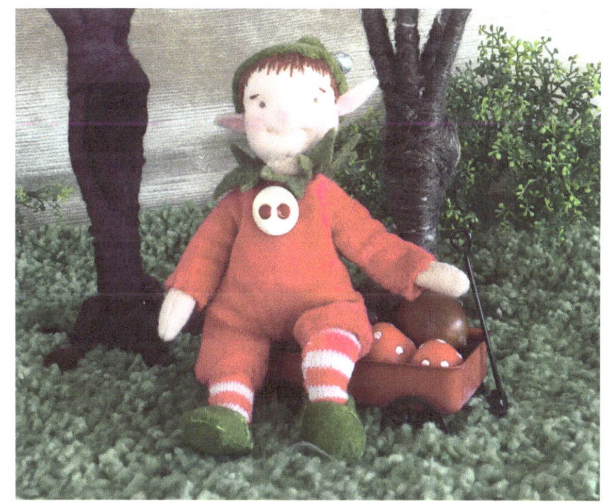

For elf shoes, cut two elf shoe soles, two elf shoe backs, and two elf shoe tops out of wool felt.

1. With two strands of matching floss, sew the short side of the shoe back to the shoe top with a tiny blanket stitch.

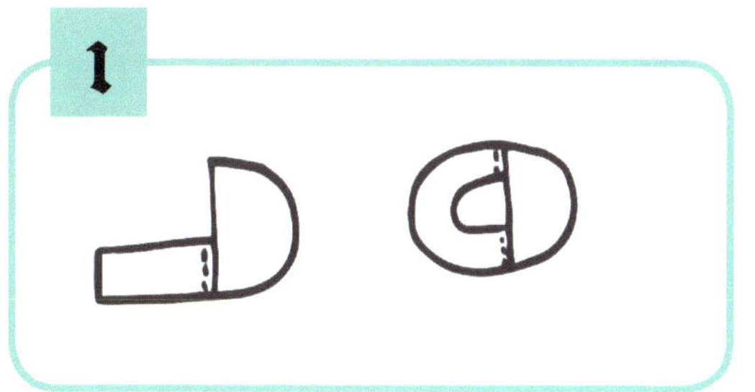

2. With a tiny blanket stitch, sew the shoe sole to the shoe top and back. Make sure you make a right and left shoe!

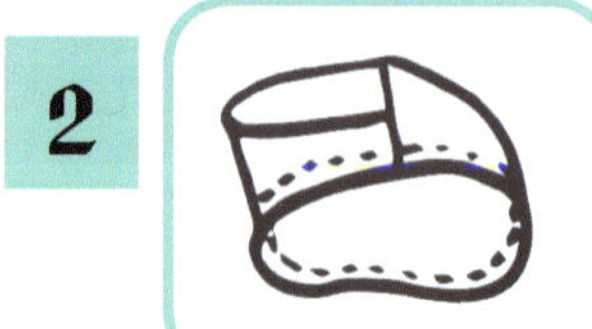

Slip shoes onto faerie.

For the pointy hat, cut one hat pattern out of cotton plush velour. Fold the hat in half and sew the curved seam with a 1/8" seam allowance. Turn right side out. Add a jingle bell or glittery bead to the point if wanted. Stitch hat onto faerie's head.

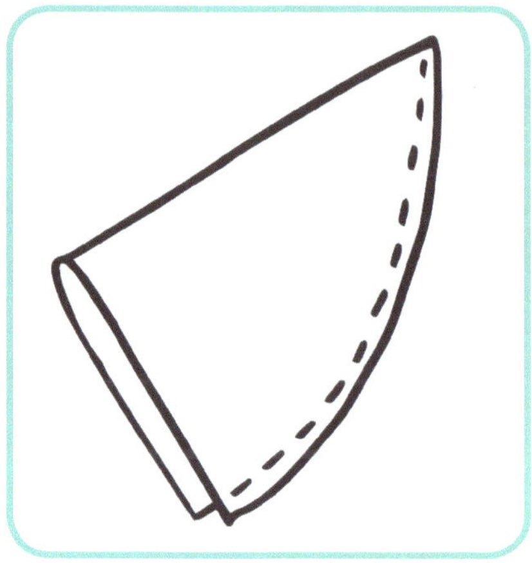

To make the faerie pants and tunic use a ⅛" seam allowance.

Cut two faerie pants out of woven wool.

1. With right sides together (RST), stitch the outside seams of the pants.
2. With RST, sew the inseam of the pants.
3. Turn pants right side out. With a tiny blanket stitch, sew hem edge of pant legs. Set aside.

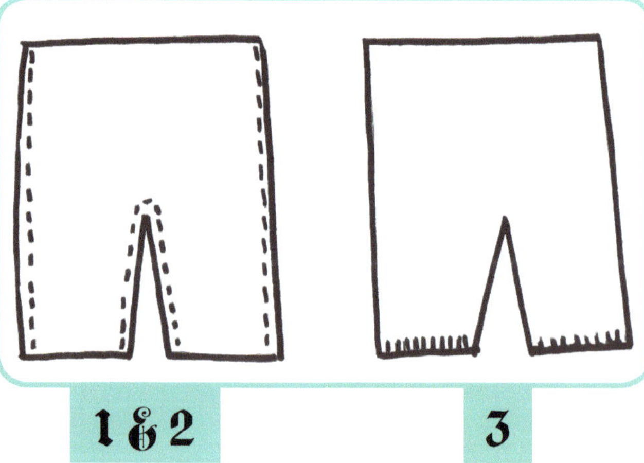

1 & 2

3

For the undershirt, cut 1/4" wide strips of muslin or cotton.

4. Starting at the wrist, wrap a strip up the arm. Continue wrapping around chest, criss-crossing around the neck to make a "collar".

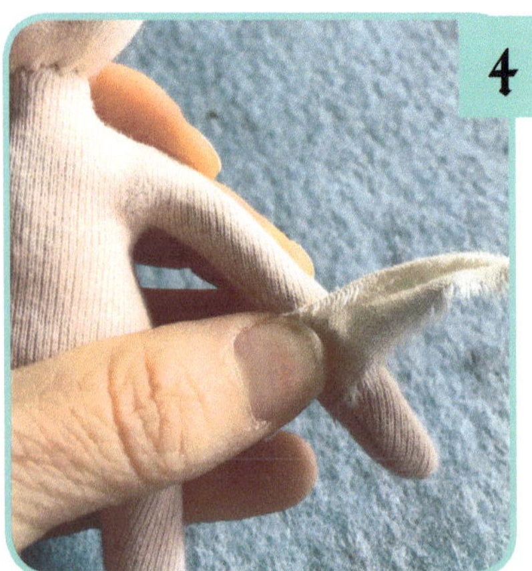

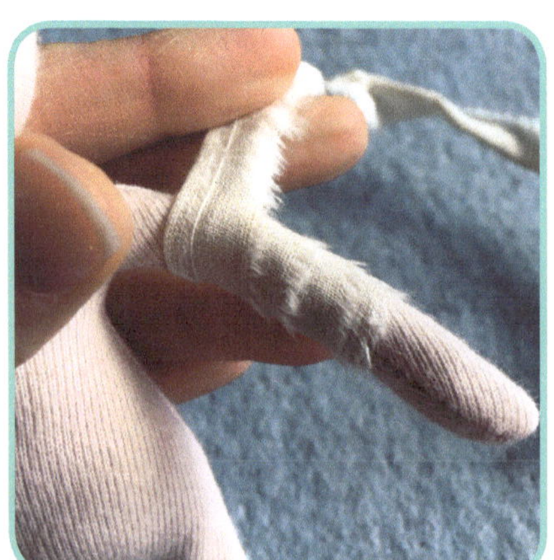

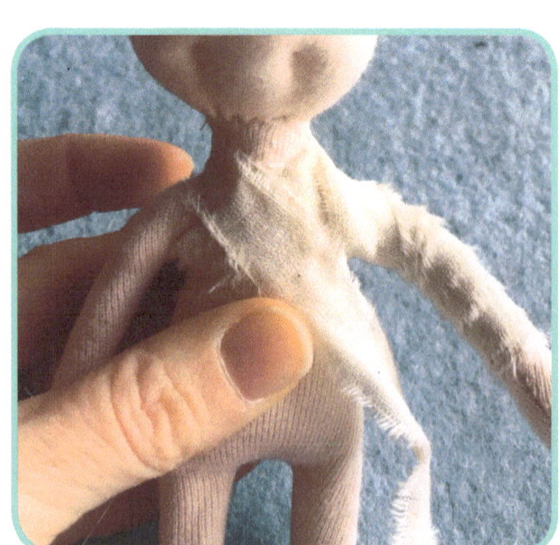

5. Stitch in place, then take another strip and wrap second arm, following the previous steps. Continue wrapping until the torso is clothed and stitch end in place.

6. Cut the tunic out of wool felt. Cut a decorative edge on the bottom hem and on edge of sleeve using pinking shears or your scissors. Embroider the front around the neck.

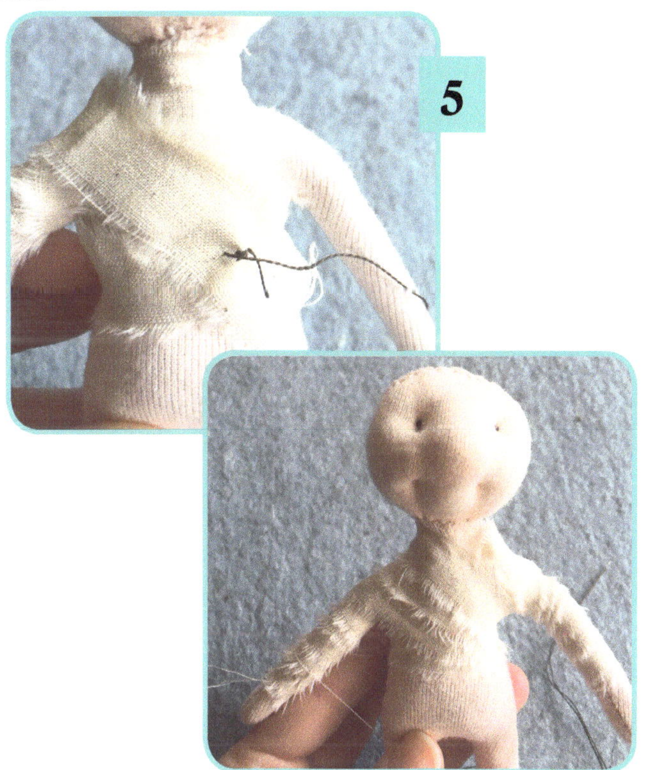

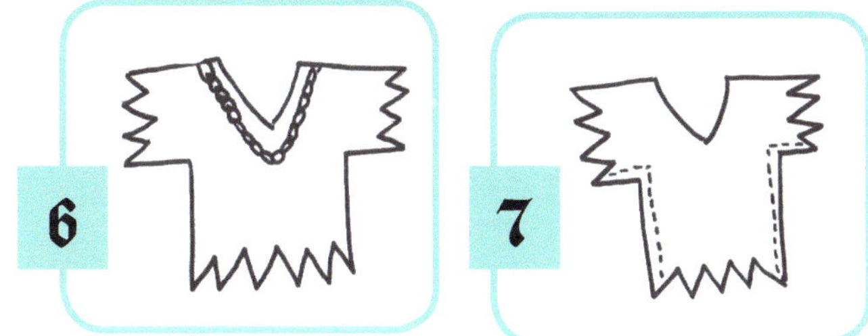

7. Slip tunic onto your faerie. Stitch together the underarm and side body seams.

8. For the faerie boots, Cut two soles and two boot tops from wool felt.

9. Fold one boot in half and sew the center seam starting at the point of the toe and continuing to the dot shown on pattern.

10. Match boot sole to shoe and with a tiny blanket stitch, sew sole onto boot. Slip shoe onto faerie's foot and fold down the top of the boot.

11. For the wool felt bag cut two bag sides and a rectangle 1" wide by 3" long for the bag body, and one bag strap ¼" wide by 5¾" long. Using a tiny blanket stitch, sew the edges of the bag strap to reinforce wool.

12. Using a tiny blanket stitch, sew the bag sides to the bag.

13. Sew the bag strap to the bag side, inside the bag.

14. Fold the bag top over. Stitch to keep in place. Add a decorative element if desired.

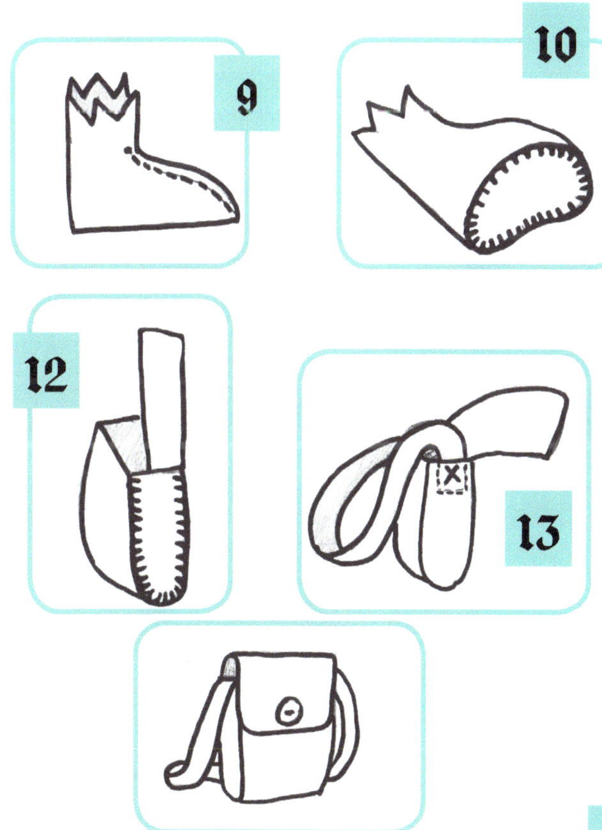

To add the wings to your faerie, pinch the excess film at the center of the wing and sew to the back of the tunic or jumper with matching thread.

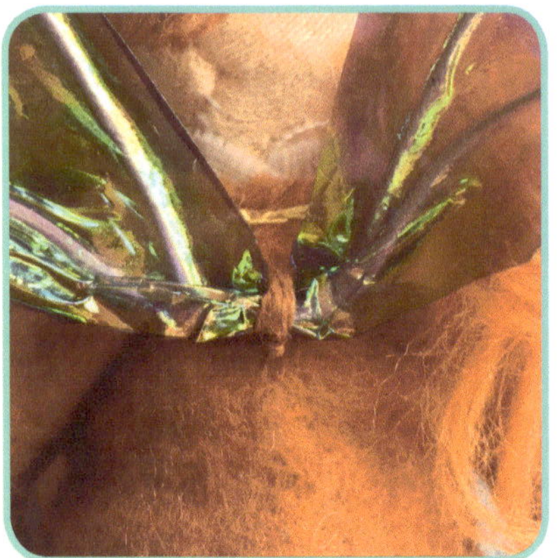

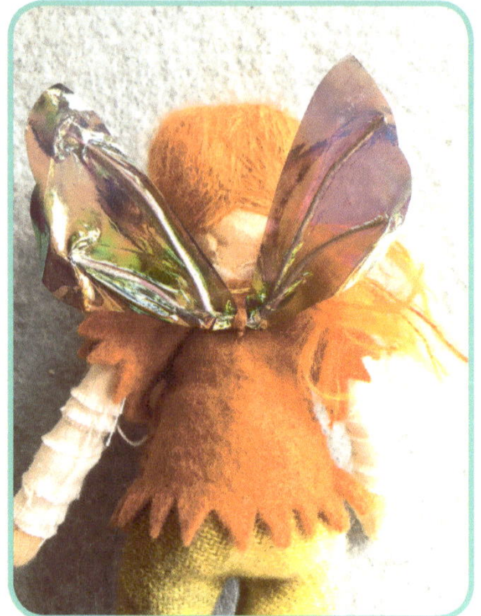

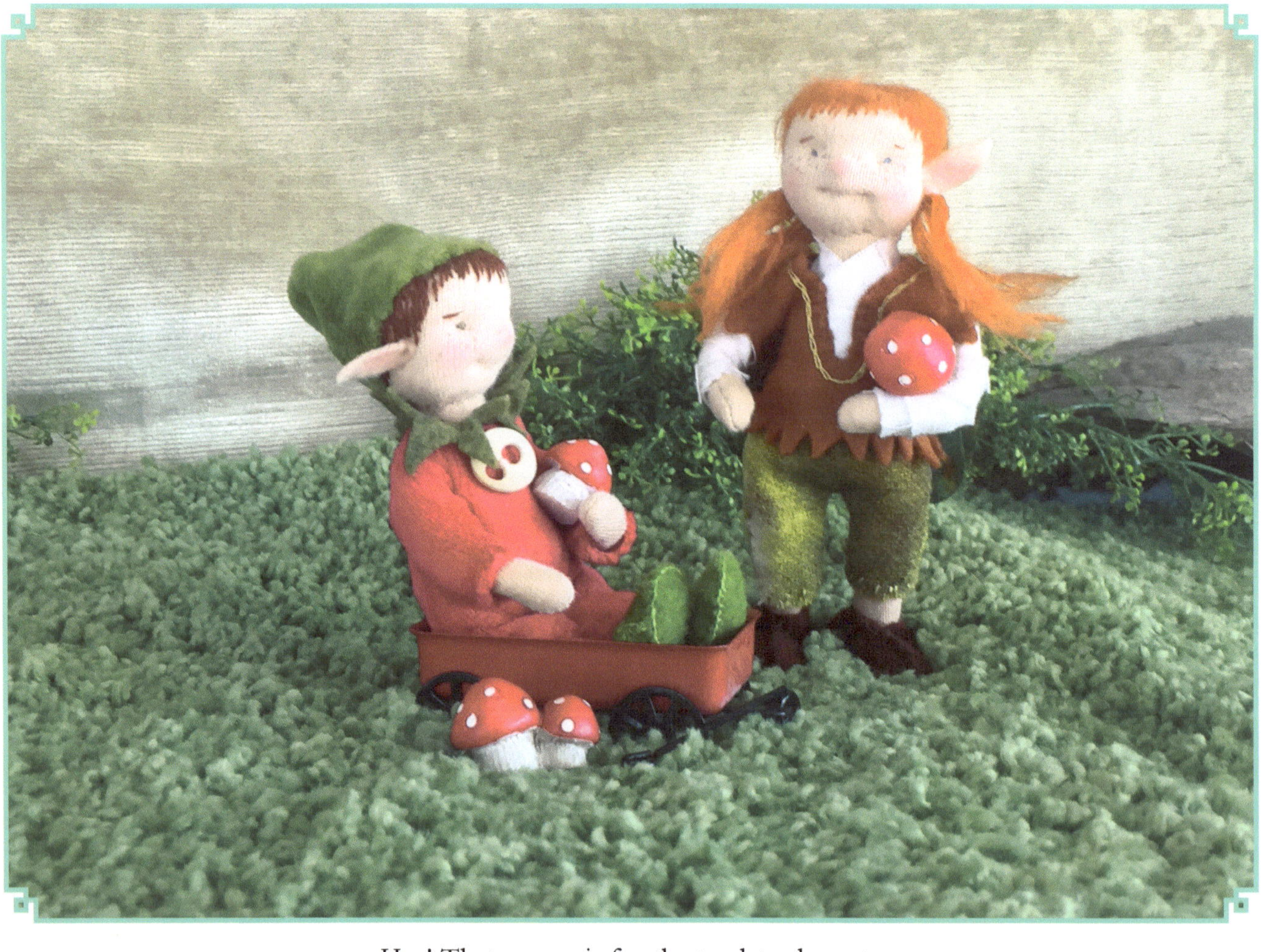

Hey! That wagon is for the toadstools, not you.

The Patterns

The following pages contain the patterns for every project in this book. They are all full size, no need to enlarge. However, you do have permission to enlarge the patterns if you choose, for personal use only.

Happy Creating!

Jennifer

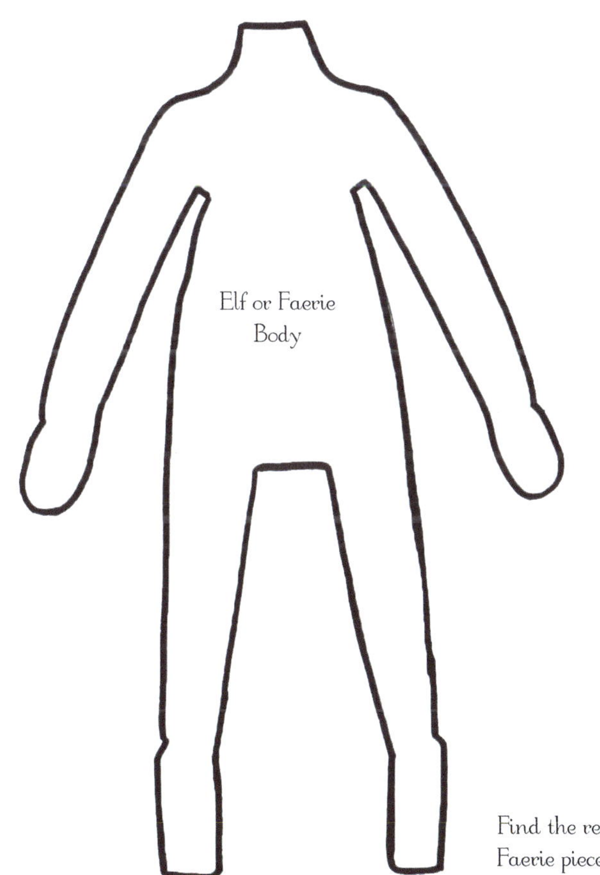

Find the rest of the Elf/ Faerie pieces on page 72

Fawn full size pattern pieces

Cutting Directons

Body–cut 2, brown felt
Ears–cut 2 white felt, 2 brown felt
Tail–cut 1 white felt, 1 brown felt
Gussets–cut one brown felt
Foot sole–cut 4 brown felt

Dragon full size pattern pieces

D

E

Match rear body piece to front body piece at notch when tracing.

G

F

*Place straight line on fold of freezer paper, trace piece. Cut out of paper and unfold for whole pattern piece.

Wing wire will emerge here

*Dragon Head Gusset

Nose end of gussett

Cutting Directons

Body–cut 2
Ears–cut 2
Gusset–cut one
Foot sole–cut 4
Wings–cut 4

**Dotted lines on wing are embroidery lines

**Dragon Wing

Dragon continued

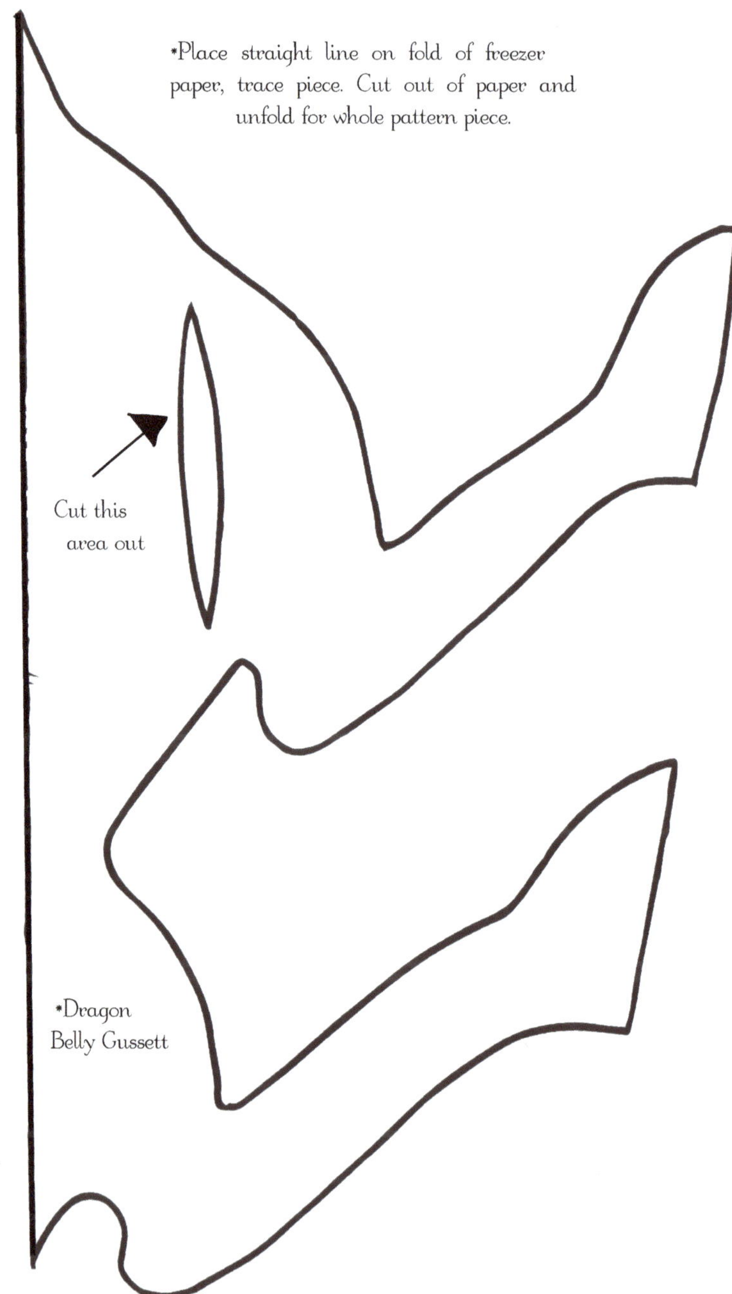

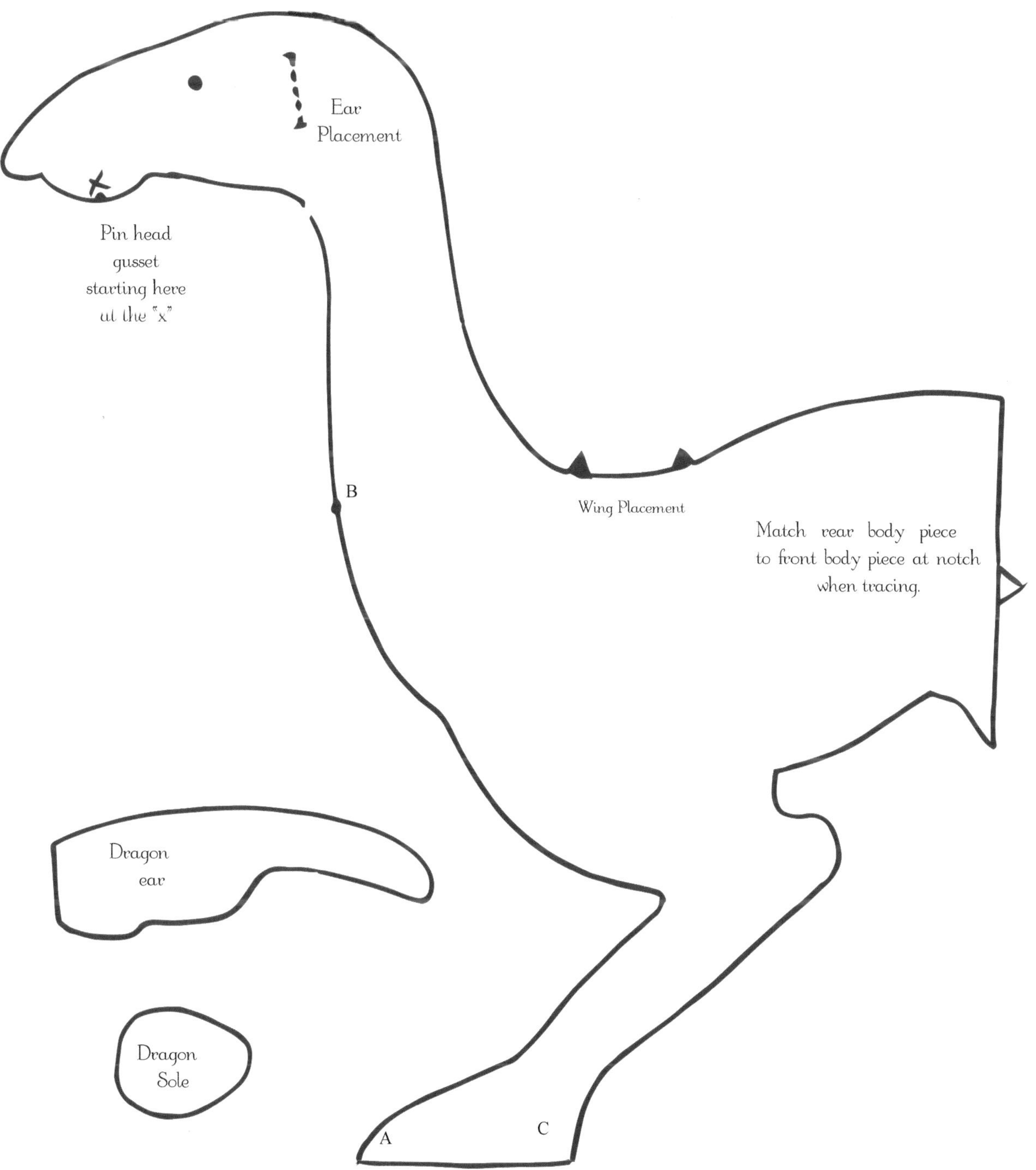
Ear
Placement
Pin head
gusset
starting here
at the "x"
B
Wing Placement
Match rear body piece
to front body piece at notch
when tracing.
Dragon
ear
Dragon
Sole
A
C

Gryphon full size pattern pieces

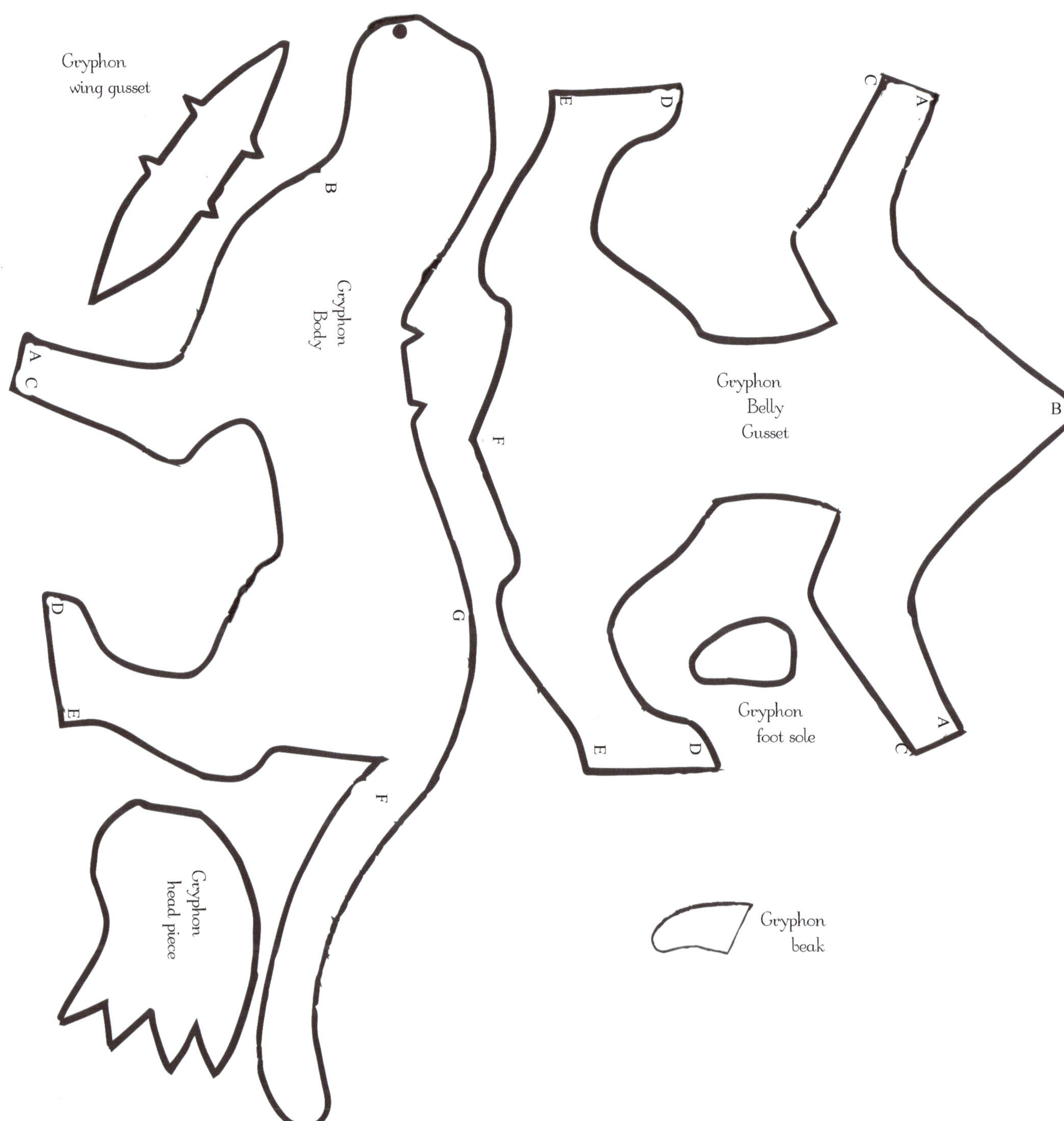

B

Gryphon wing

Gryphon wing overlay

A

Guide for Gryphon's wired foot

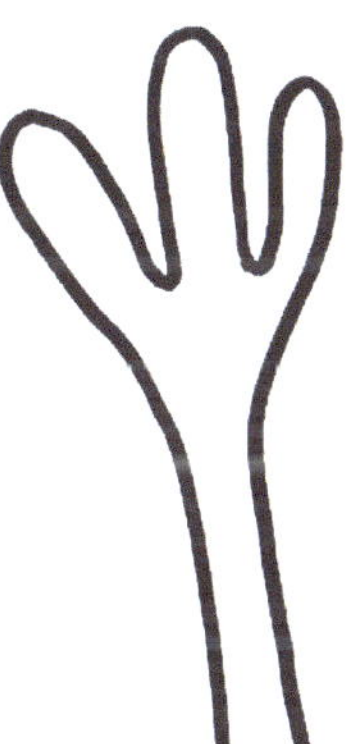

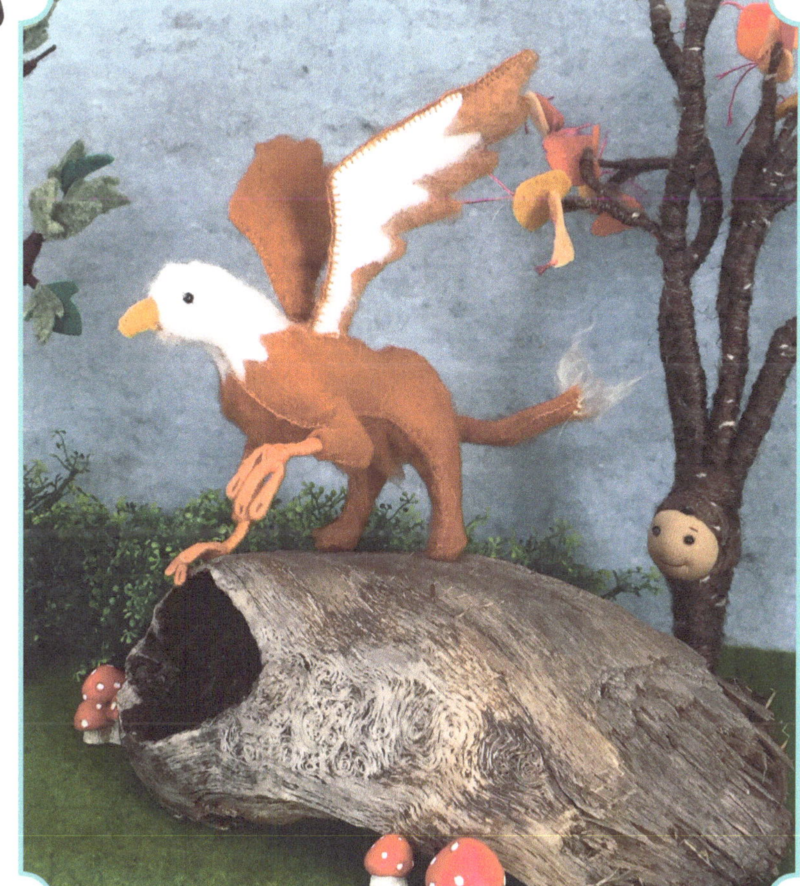

Cutting Directons

Body–cut 2, rust felt
Head piece–cut 2 ,white felt
Belly gusset–cut one, rust felt
Foot sole–cut 4, rust felt
Beak–cut 1, orange felt
Wings–cut 4 tan felt
Wing overlay–cut 2 white felt
Foot sole–cut 2, rust felt
Wing gussett–cut 1, rust felt

Knight and Tower full size pattern pieces

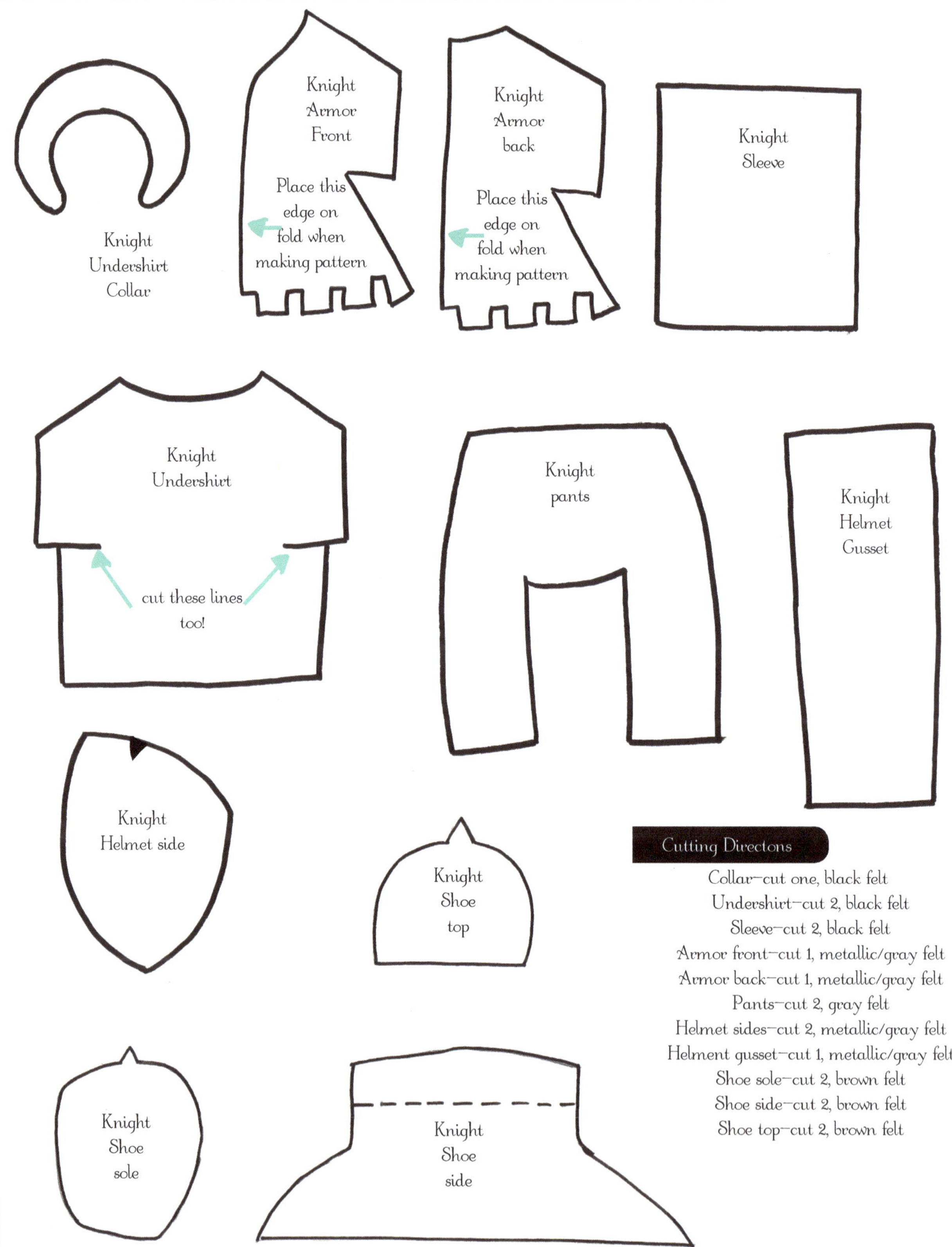

Cutting Directons

Collar–cut one, black felt
Undershirt–cut 2, black felt
Sleeve–cut 2, black felt
Armor front–cut 1, metallic/gray felt
Armor back–cut 1, metallic/gray felt
Pants–cut 2, gray felt
Helmet sides–cut 2, metallic/gray felt
Helment gusset–cut 1, metallic/gray felt
Shoe sole–cut 2, brown felt
Shoe side–cut 2, brown felt
Shoe top–cut 2, brown felt

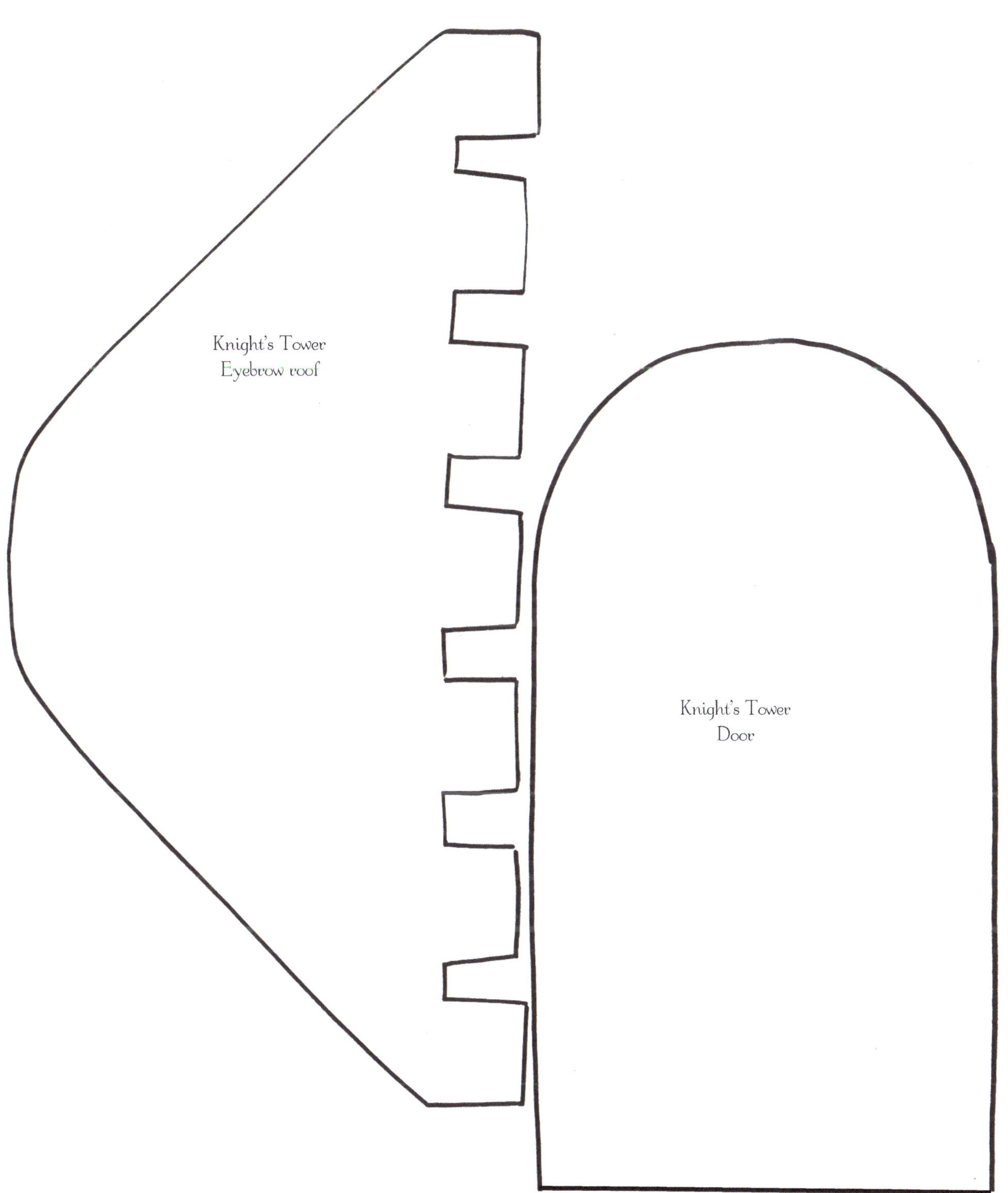
Knight's Tower
Eyebrow roof
Knight's Tower
Door

Knight's Tower continued

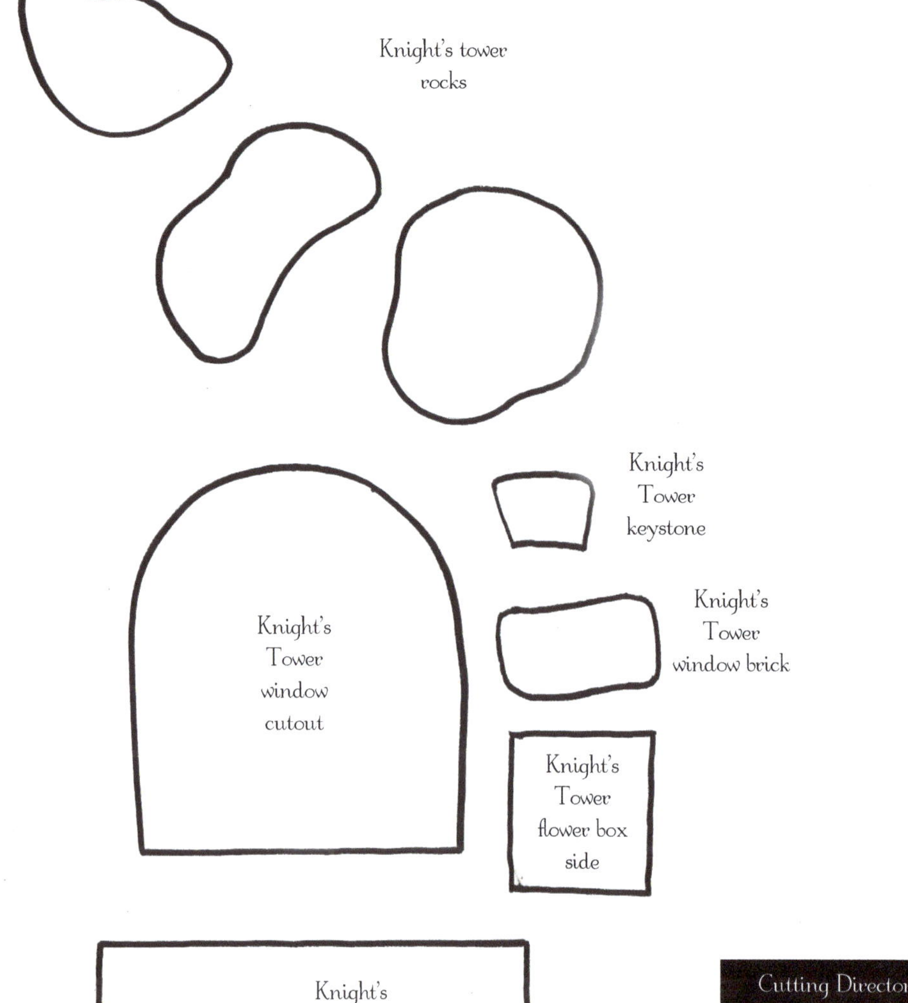

Cutting Directons

Tower wall–cut 2 following directions on page 42
Eyebrow roof– cut 2, gray felt
Coat of Arms Shield–cut 1, red felt
Door– cut 2, brown felt
Stones–cut 6 total, or more if you prefer, mottled light tan felt
Keystone–cut 1, mottled tan felt
Window Bricks–cut 9, mottled tan felt
Flower box– cut 3, brown felt
Flower box sides–cut 4, brown felt
*Tower roof–cut 1, brown felt, cut 1 dark brown felt

*if desired, cut 3 window bricks (or more!) out of brown felt for roof shingles

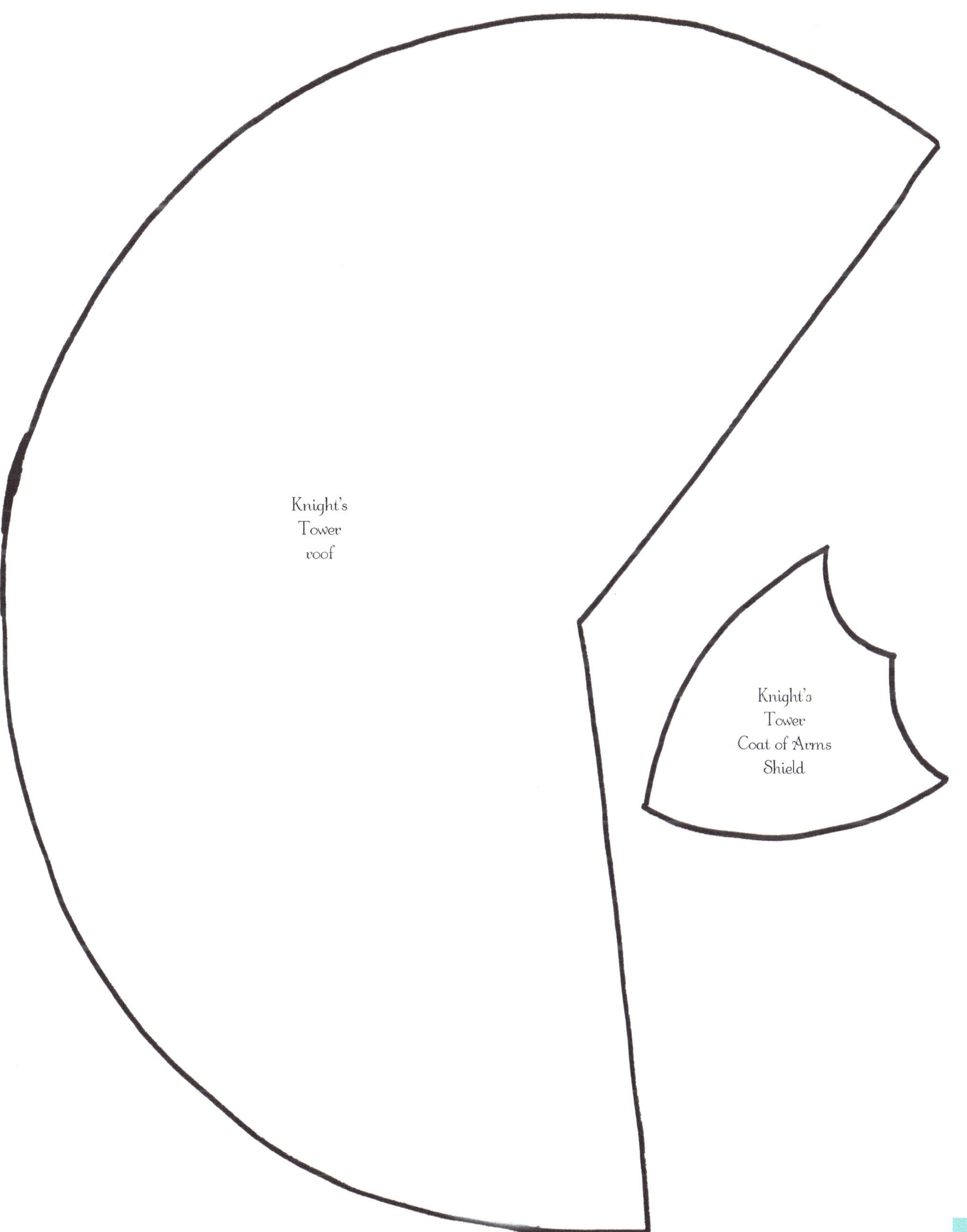
Knight's
Tower
roof
Knight's
Tower
Coat of Arms
Shield

Elves & Faeries full size pattern pieces

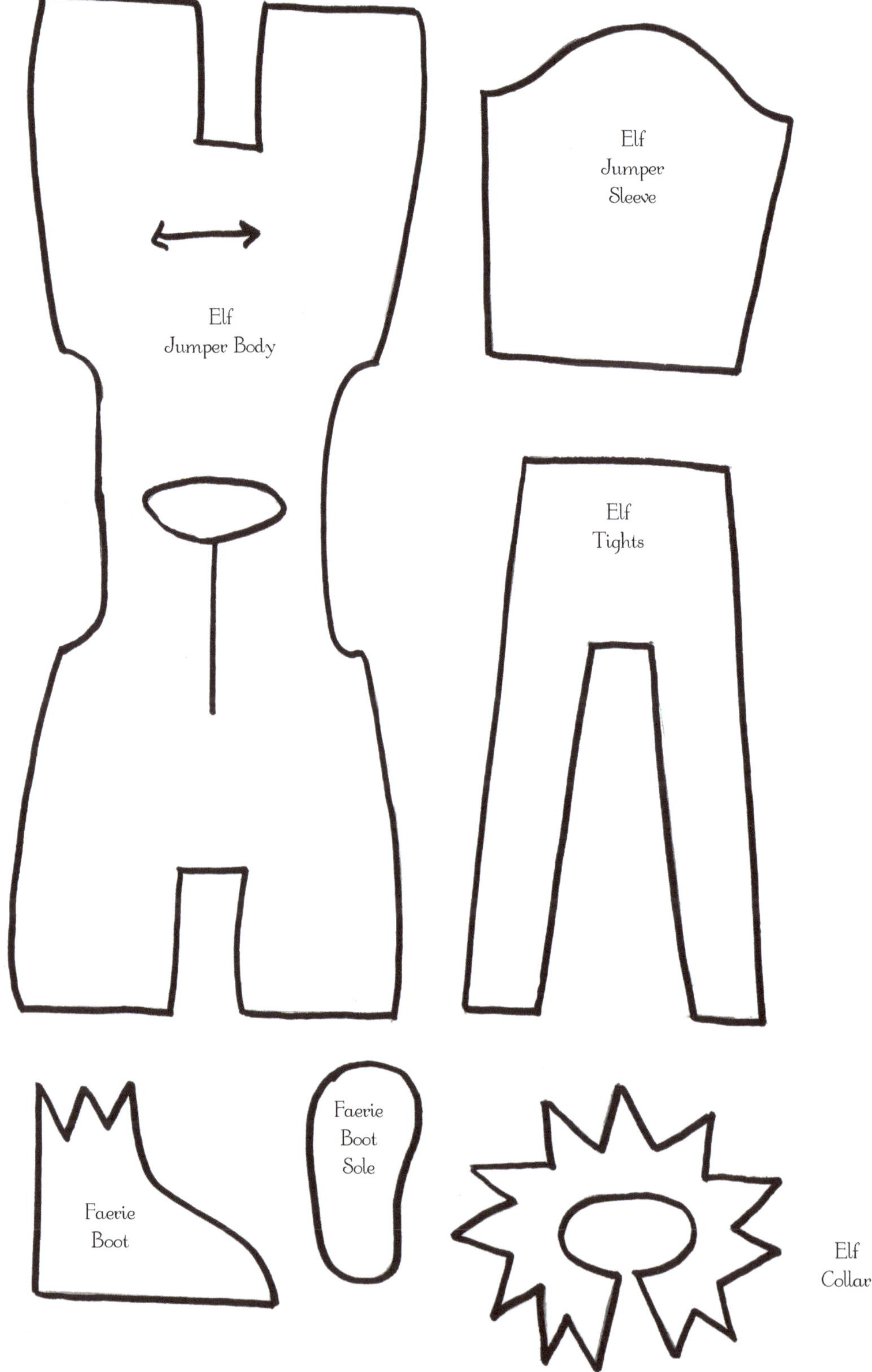

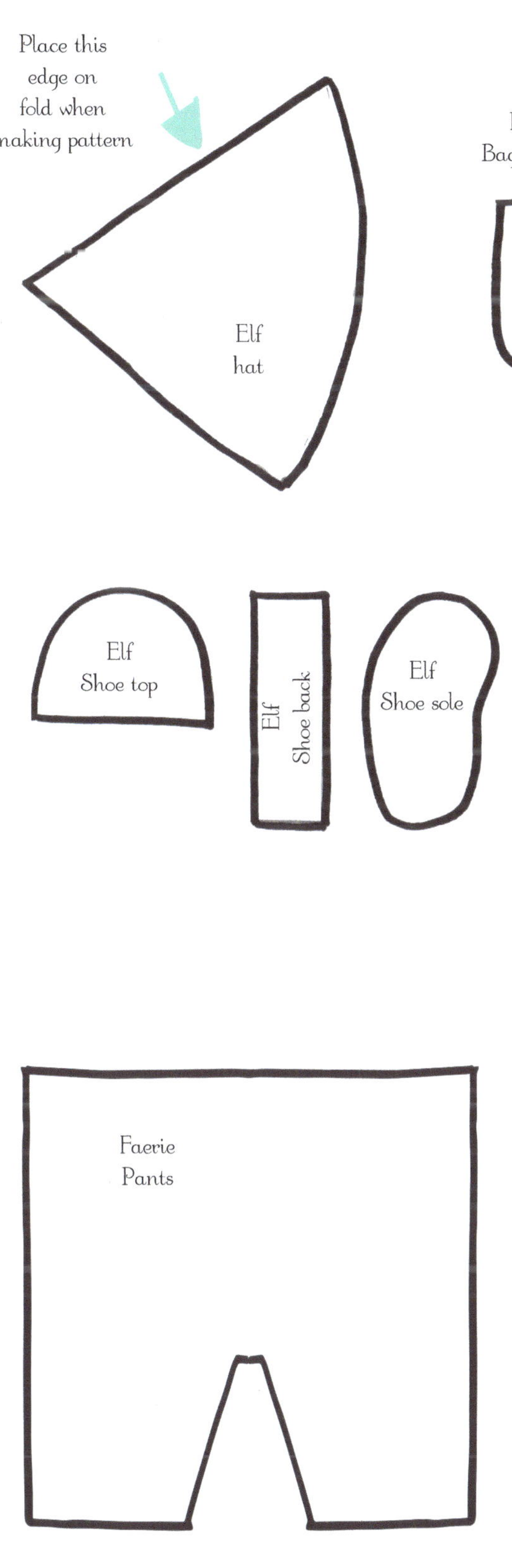

Cutting Directons

Jumper Body–cut 1 from cotton velour
Jumper sleeve–cut 2 from cotton velour
Tights–cut 2 from cotton knit
Faerie Boot–cut 2 from wool felt
Faerie Boot Sole–cut 2 from wool felt
Collar–cut 1 from wool felt
Hat–cut 1 on fold from cotton velour
Bag side– cut 2 from wool felt
Bag body–cut 1 rectangle 1" x 3" from wool felt
Bag Strap–cut 1 strip 1/4" x 5 3/4" from wool felt
Elf Shoe top–cut 2 from wool felt
Elf Shoe back–cut 2 from wool felt
Elf Shoe sole–cut 2 from wool felt
Pants–cut 2 from woven wool
Tunic–cut 1 from wool felt
•Elf or Faerie Body–DO NOTCUT! See directions on page 49

•Elf or Faerie Body pattern piece can be found on page 61.

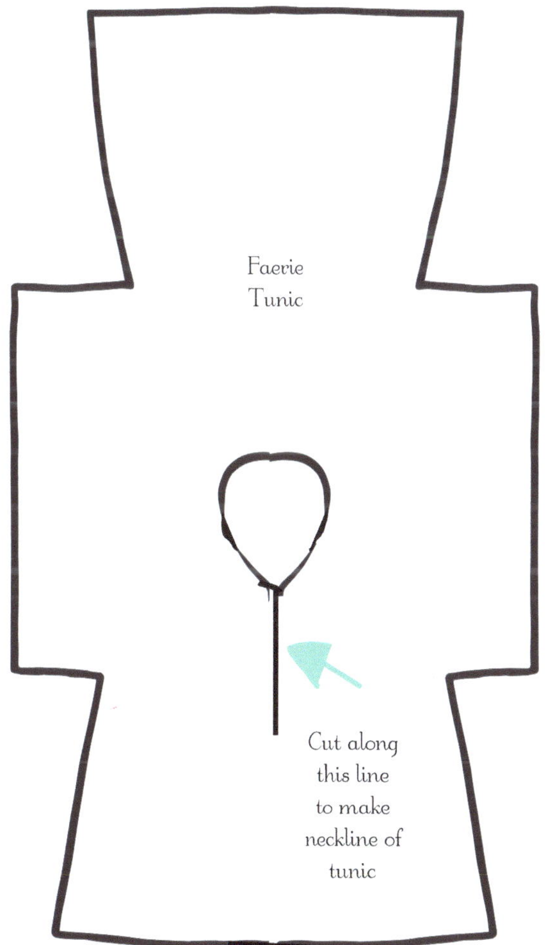

Suppliers & Resources

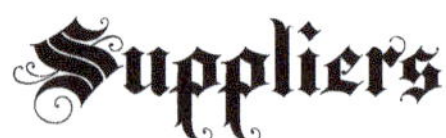

Retailers in the United States and on-line

The Dragon Charmer
www.thedragoncharmer.com
The Dragon Charmer carries figure cord, bendy dolls, binding thread, sewing patterns for other posable toys, kits, supplies, and more. Subscribe to the newsletter for free sewing patterns!

Weir Crafts
www.weircrafts.com
Weir Crafts carries just about everything you need to make Waldorf dolls, including: wool felt, cotton interlock knit, cotton plush velour, cotton gauze, hair yarn, cotton pipe cleaners, and more!

Doll Makers Journey
www.dollmakersjourney.com
Doll Maker's Journey carries a variety of doll making supplies, including: stuffing tools, tiny turning tubes, air erasable marking pens, Prismacolor pencils, and more.

National Non-Wovens
Wool felt and wool blend felts in an amazing array of colors.
For a retailer near you visit:
www.nationalnonwovens.com/Applications/craft/franny.html#Retail

Sassy Bears
http://sassybears.com/
Sassy Bears carries lovely mohair for making wigs that you don't have to knit or crochet yourself, as well as sew on eyes, tiny buttons, and lace.

The Felt Pod
www.thefeltpod.com
Metallic felt for the knight, plus thicker 3mm felts for the tower walls and for brushable animals!

A Child's Dream
https://achildsdream.com
All kinds of supplies for fiber arts and Waldorf doll making, including bendy doll bodies, fabrics, threads, and more.

Retailers in Canada an online

Bear Dance Crafts
http://www.beardancecrafts.com
Everything you need to make Waldorf dolls including: bendy dolls, cotton interlock knit, hair, wool felt, cotton gauze and more!

Hamels Fabrics and Quilting
https://www.hamelsfabrics.com
They carry a variety of colors of the Genziana wool thread.

Retailers in the UK and Beyond

Little Oke Dolls
https://waldorfdolls.co.uk/
Just about everything you could need for Waldorf doll making! Plus the owner is super friendly and helpful.

DeWitte Engel
https://www.dewitteengel.nl.en
They carry the figure cord, as well as wool felt in many different thicknesses, cotton interlock knit, bendy dolls, cotton plush velour, wool felt balls, and more!

To purchase directly from them go to:https://mijn.witteengel.nl
It is all in Dutch at the moment, but they are working on translating it to English and other languages. Handily, they have incorporated a Google Translate button which will help you find what you are looking for.

Resources:

Making your first Waldorf doll head: https://www.youtube.com/watch?v=cjemIHXz0rA&t=13s

Making wool felt beads
https://www.youtube.com/watch?v=DGoWTI3IJdA

Sewing in your Dragon's wing gusset
https://youtu.be/LyN1u01Apm8

Wrapping the limbs of your Dryad
https://youtu.be/GwUfr3JJOAA

Making a Sturdy Neck for your Waldorf Dolls
https://youtu.be/44pgKMG3hCw

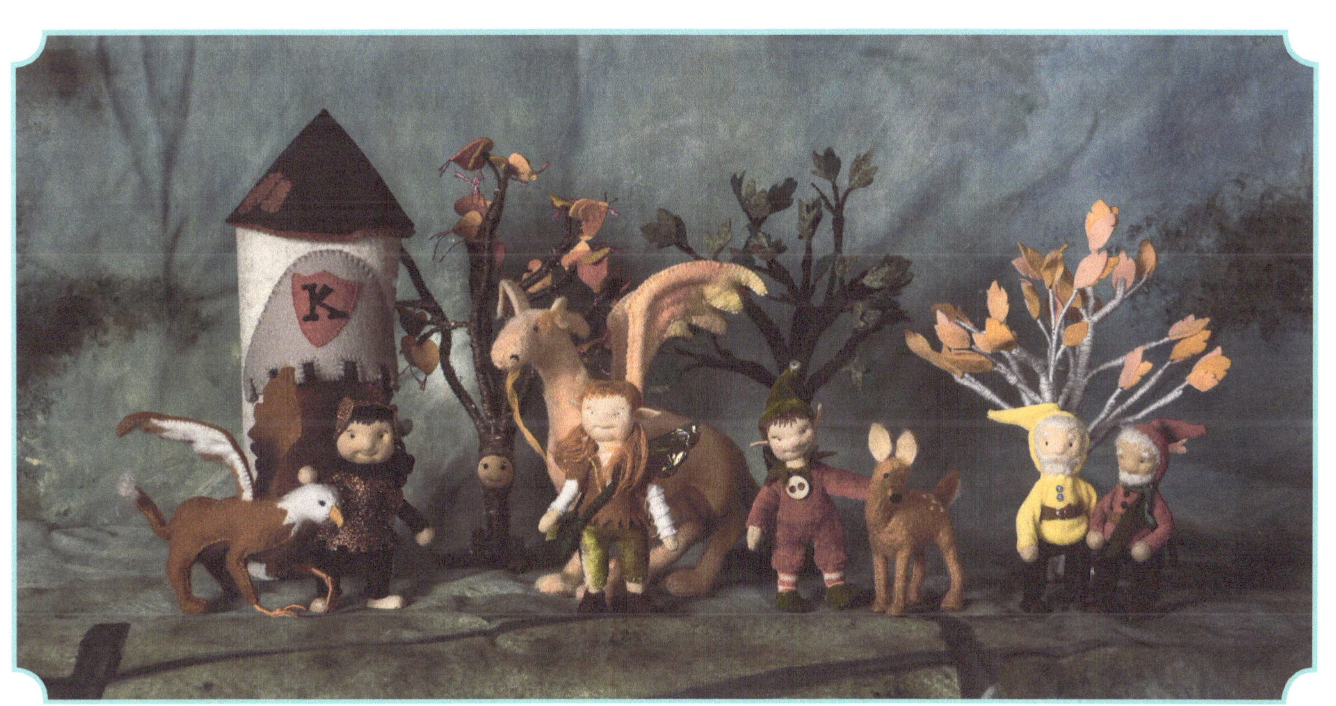

About the Author

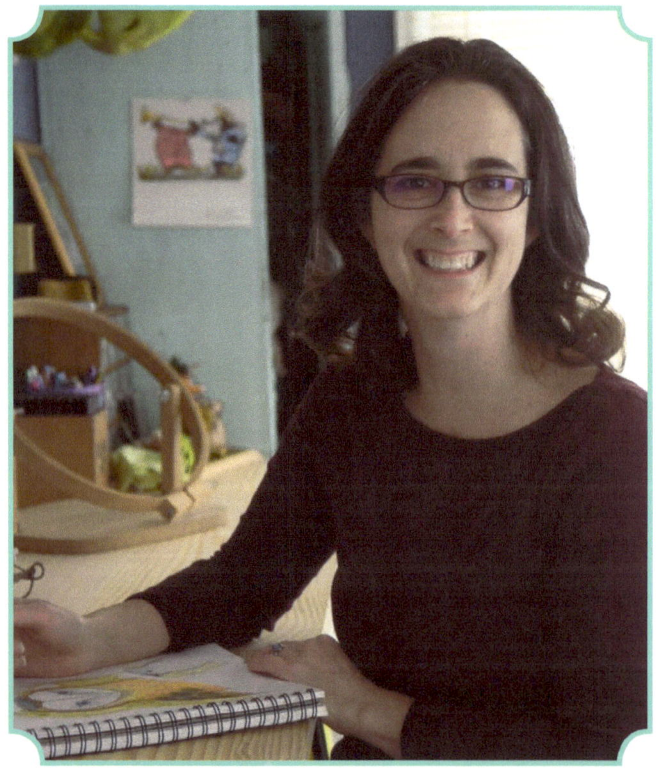

Jennifer Carson lives in Michigan with her husband, four sons, and many four legged friends. She grew up on a steady diet of Muppet movies and renaissance faires. Occasionally her parents would catch her reading under the blankets with a flashlight, but most of the time she got away with it!

All that reading fed her very large imagination. Besides creating creatures, she also publishes fantasy tales for young and old, is a playwright, a managing editor for a local magazine, and is always coming up with more ideas to bring magick into your every day.

Visit her online at:

thedragoncharmer.com

Other books by Jennifer Carson:

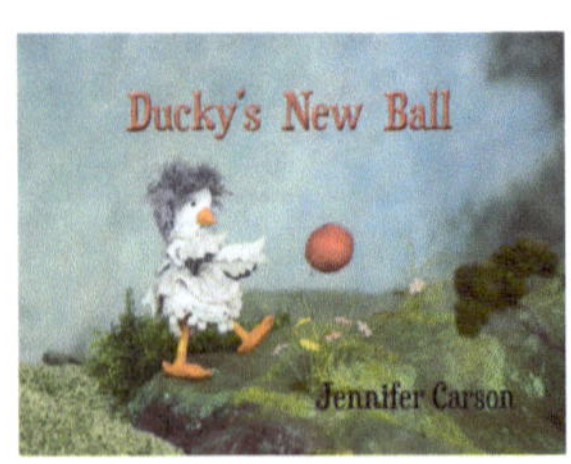

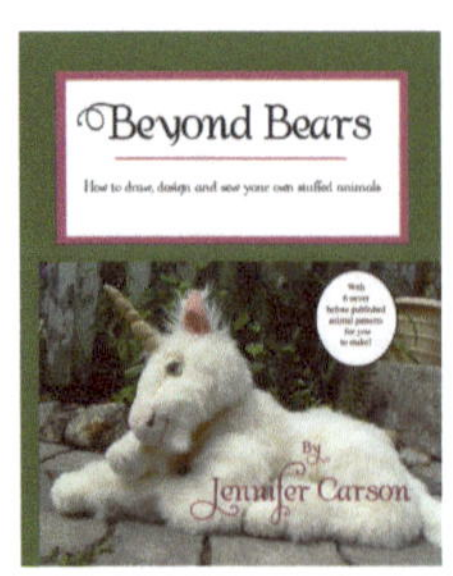

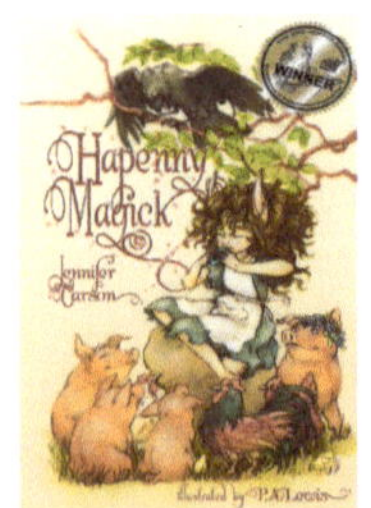

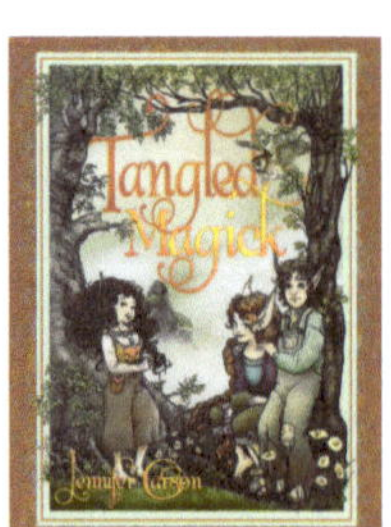

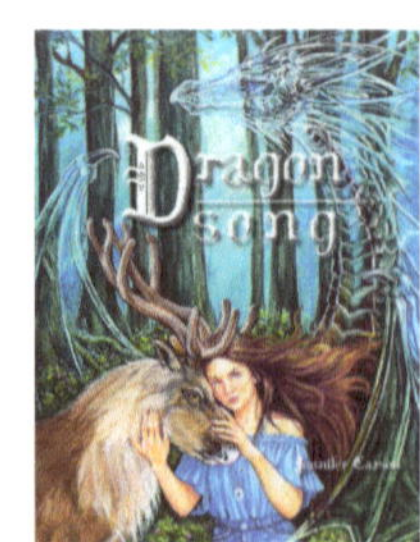

All of Jennifer's books are available to order at your favorite bookstore, online, or through her website, www.thedragoncharmer.com

www.ingramcontent.com/pod-product-compliance
Lightning Source LLC
LaVergne TN
LVHW070510120826
845147LV00031BA/556
9781622510412